THE
LEVERAGED
Business

How You Can Go from Overwhelmed
at Six Figures to Seven Figures
(and Get Your Life Back)

FABIENNE FREDRICKSON

This book is being given to

_____ ,

because I care about you and your greater success,

from

_____

Advance Praise for
The Leveraged Business

"Using the principles outlined in these pages, I reached Seven Figures in one year! Learning the Leveraged Business Activators is a must-have in growing and scaling your business. Thanks Fabienne for your astute business insight." —Aysha Treadwell

"Fabienne Fredrickson is a walking testimonial that you can have a seven-figure business, a thriving marriage, and be a wonderful mom. I'm thrilled to see this methodology launched into the world for more people to be impacted by her business methods. Don't miss this book! Your life will be forever impacted and will never be the same when you discover how to leverage your business and get your life back."
—Jen Hickle

"The Leveraged Business book is worth tens of thousands of dollars. Literally! The reason: Fabienne describes the same proven strategies and mindset shifts that she teaches in her Leveraged Business program that I attended. And her strategies do work! Everything that I have applied has worked for me and I have achieved tremendous business growth for the past four years."
—Alexander Nikolov

"Reading this book gave me the tools I needed to see the growth I was looking for in my business. I was operating by the seat of my pants and now I have a fabulous team to back me up, systems, a marketing plan, more time for fun, and increased revenues. Wow! I couldn't put it down!! Every business owner should read it!" —Judy Heft

"Fabienne is a transformational business coach. There is so much truth in shifting your mindset and working the Eight Activators. My business and life are three hundred times better and more balanced due to her method. Ready to be the best person and boss you can be? Dive in!" —Denise Allan

"Brilliant! Fabienne is honest about the entrepreneurial journey. Bold but loving about the exact steps to move from overwhelm to exponential growth. Even one of these Activators will create exponential growth when implemented." —Nettie Owens

"I just finished reading The Leveraged Business, and it is spot-on and a must-read for any business owner who wants the coveted work-life balance. This book isn't just a theory about it; it provides the practical steps to make it happen once and for all."
—Lorry Leigh Belhumeur, Ph.D.

"Fabienne combines genius and heart. The alchemy is brilliant wisdom to help leverage all aspects of a business. I am grateful for the practical wisdom and strategies in this book!" —Julie Reisler

"Fabienne is a genius. If you want to soar to greatness fast, get this book. It's all here and the resources are the icing on the cake! She's the real deal. Using just a few of her concepts has made my business bigger, bolder, more authentic, and more cash-infused! I sleep through the night now too!" —Raeleen St. Pierre

"A must-read for every entrepreneur who wants to create the financial resources in order to have a bigger impact in the world, while still having a life." —Rucsandra Mitrea

Contents

Free Resources

Before you dive into the Eight Leveraged Business Activators, I recommend the following valuable (and free) resources to help you as you read this book.

Your Cheat Sheet for the Eight Activators

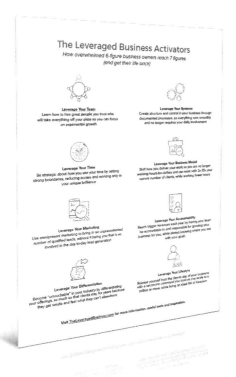

Sometimes, seeing the entire system on a single page helps you understand the full picture, and the journey ahead of you.

If you would enjoy having the Leveraged Business Activators cheat sheet for easy reference, you can download this infographic on **www. TheLeveragedBusiness.com**.

The Leveraged Business Assessment

You may be wondering just how leveraged *your* business is, or where you are currently on the path to growth. Understanding your progress will help you see the way forward.

The Leveraged Business Assessment will show you where you are now, what's currently getting in the way of more fully leveraging your business, and where you can improve.

Find the assessment on **www.TheLeverageAssessment.com.** Going through this helpful process takes five minutes, and we'll email your results to you.

Free Exploratory Strategy Call

Scaling your business can be lonely. Not everyone understands your vision, and few people have experience leveraging a business. We understand firsthand the value of talking through your company's situation with someone qualified—especially when it involves creating an actionable twenty-four-month plan to overcome any obstacles to success.

We are here to provide this support, at no cost to you, as a thank-you for buying this book. If you'd like to schedule this exploratory strategy session, simply answer a few questions at **www.TheLeveragedBusiness.com**

You don't need to go it alone. I've personally trained our Strategy Coaches to compassionately assist you in discovering what's not working in your business now, where you'd like to be in twenty-four months, and what your customized plan of action can be to get there.

We can also answer your questions about the Leveraged Business program, and how it can help you implement your plan with structure, accountability, and a community of like-minded entrepreneurs who are also on the journey to a leveraged business.

The strategy session is completely free for qualified business owners, who make 80K a year or more in revenues or a minimum of 8K a month consistently.

We are here to serve you. When it feels right—whether it's now, or in a few chapters, or once you've reached the last page of this book—schedule your free exploratory strategy session: **www.TheLeveragedBusiness.com.**

Preface

How to Know If This Book Is for You

People in your life see you and think, "That person has got it going on." You're smart; you always have been. You're good at what you do, and your clients like you. Some of them even love you. In fact, you're a high-achieving superstar in other people's eyes (even if you don't always feel like it). You've experienced some success in your business, maybe more than you initially thought you would. In fact, if you were to measure backward to where you first started, you would be pretty proud of yourself for what you've accomplished so far, even if you'd like to be farther ahead.

But if we're being honest, *you're also overwhelmed*.

You've got clients, some of them good clients, but they don't always show up when they say they will, or pay you on time. And sometimes they make unreasonable requests, and you don't know how to say no to them. The to-do list is never-ending and it seems like you'll never catch up. You've got a few people helping you, but truth be told, you've never thought of yourself as a good manager, so working with them is another headache you didn't anticipate.

The people supporting you don't always understand what you want—or do it right—so you end up doing many tasks yourself, because it would take longer to explain it to others than to just get it done yourself.

You initially got a lot of your business through word of mouth, but with all of your current expenses, you find it difficult to grow further, because there's just no more time.

You know you need systems to run your business better, but you just don't know where to start. Creating them from scratch and overseeing them feels like the last thing you want to do.

It's all so overwhelming. There's so much to figure out, and you're stretched pretty thin.

Where to find good people, and how to keep them?

How to delegate to the people you've brought on board?

How to generate more cash flow when there's so little time?

How to charge more without losing clients?

How to become better at marketing your business?

How to create systems so things don't fall through the cracks?

How to make the most of the limited time you have?

How to make a dent in your to-do list?

How to figure out if the clients you're targeting are the right ones?

How to make sense of social media and use it to grow your business?

How to turn off work in the evenings and spend quality time with those you love?

How to actually take a vacation without everything falling apart? . . .

You know your business should run more smoothly, but everything still depends on you right now, because no one can do the work quite like you—and frankly, deep down, you don't really trust anyone to do it right. And who has the time to train someone else, anyway?

All of this makes you feel pretty frustrated.

After all the hard work you've put in (the long evenings at the computer after dinner, the perseverance, the sleepless nights, not being able to take a vacation without bringing your laptop to check in), you honestly thought you'd be further along by now.

Your income has grown, yes, but so have your problems. You're working harder than ever, but you feel like you're not making as much money as you should be. And let's face it, *growth sucks cash*—you don't always have the cash flow to do the things you want to do with the business.

A while back, you had big visions for your business, but now you keep getting stuck, taking a whack-a-mole approach to keeping up, and you don't feel like you're being all that strategic.

You're feeling impatient because success isn't coming fast enough. Privately, you sometimes wonder if this whole "being self-employed" thing is really worth the effort; in your darkest moments you dream of scaling back the business (or even going to work for someone else, even though you're now completely unemployable!).

You're operating solo, in uncharted territory, without a plan. You feel isolated, and sometimes miss working with other people, toward a common goal, with all the camaraderie that comes along with that. And even though you've got some help these days, it's just not the same. It's lonely doing everything yourself.

You have some idea of where you want to go, but you're caught up in the realities of everyday life, and you don't really know how to get from here to there.

Somehow, you still feel a glimmer of hope. The dream is there underneath all the layers of overwhelm. You dream of fulfilling a potential or a calling that is quietly nagging at you. You want a greater level of happiness and flexibility—even the freedom to take a truly unplugged vacation!

You dream of making a bigger impact, having greater financial security, paying yourself more, and having a real chance at wealth creation. And, of course, you want to feel confident again.

If this is you, here's what you need to do now to find relief and gain significant momentum in your business, without compromising your life:

Leverage.

When you leverage different aspects of your business, you create a business that effectively manages itself—that not only scales without you needing to do much, but also allows you to grow your income and get your life back.

Regardless of your country, your gender, the size of your business, or the type of industry you work in, there are systemic causes for entrepreneurial overwhelm at the six-figure level—the ones you are experiencing right now. These systemic issues are preventing your growth, financial and otherwise. But it doesn't have to be this way.

You've invested so much of your time, and of yourself, into this venture. Now is not the time to give up, especially if you understand that your issues are fixable. People fix their businesses at this level all the time.

The secret? What got you *here* is not what's going to get you *there.*

Leverage is the simple solution to any stagnation, overwhelm, or frustration you are experiencing.

What Is Leverage?

The concept of Leverage is related to the principle of levers in physics. You can use a lever to lift objects that would otherwise be too heavy to pick up. In business, leverage is the ability to multiply the outcome of one's efforts without a corresponding increase in input. In other words, leverage is *the act of increasing results without putting in more effort.*

Better results, less effort.

What a Leveraged Business Looks Like

Jane was a lifelong corporate employee. She produced great results for a well-known luxury organization, but at the expense of her health. For decades she worked ungodly hours, consistently putting the needs of the corporation before her own. After many years of giving her all, she left, and applied her extensive human resources expertise to start her own HR and executive coaching firm, consulting for other corporations.

With her stellar reputation and exceptional networking skills, Jane got clients right away, and quickly brought her business to 10K a month. (A note on usage: in this case, *K* stands for thousands of dollars, but I intentionally omit mentions of currency throughout the book, because the tenets of a leveraged business are universal and our members span the globe.) But by the time I met her, at a small-business seminar, she was thinking of shutting down her business entirely.

I was puzzled. Why would she think of closing her six-figure business when it was going so well, and she was finally free of her all-consuming corporate job?

Well, Jane told me, on the outside, it looked like she had it all together. Yes, she was making Six Figures, she was newly married to the love of her life, and the corporations she consulted for were seeing positive results. But on the inside, she was overwhelmed, she underpaid herself, she was burning the candle at both ends, and she questioned whether it was worth it to keep working on evenings and weekends.

She wanted to grow, yes, but the idea of taking on more clients and having a larger team seemed to translate to more problems and longer hours for her. And she knew she didn't want that.

Jane was exhausted when she joined us in the Leveraged Business program. She doubted her ability to scale the business, and never could have imagined that she would reach 500K in revenues in a few short years. Within a couple more years, she reached the elusive million-dollar mark in her business, just by following the process outlined in these pages.

Jane now has a team of expert "mini-mes," associates who follow her process and deliver her work in the marketplace, upholding her standards. She goes on several vacations with her (now retired) husband each year, while her business is making a million in revenue.

Last week, she texted me:

"I remember that we set my goal for $175K the first year, which would mean $14K per month. I truly thought that was impossible. I am now regularly making $100K+ every month! I am so thrilled with the growth and success!!"

Embracing the mindset of a person who runs a Leveraged Business helped Jane get her business to Seven Figures (a million in revenue annually) while stepping back from its day-to-day operations. She is now making a significant impact professionally and is also enjoying life again, grateful to be self-employed.

Jane's story is not an isolated result. Throughout these pages, you'll read before-and-after case studies of people who followed the same process, with our help, and they too reached Seven Figures—while getting to enjoy their lives again.

Remember, your business's current growing pains are predictable, a rite of passage, and eminently fixable. The process you'll find in the following pages is your road map.

Enjoy, and know that we're here for you when you need us.

What to Know Before We Dive In

I HAVE HAD the privilege of meeting countless people (most of them women) at the six-figure level who feel utterly overwhelmed in their businesses and deeply frustrated that they're not moving fast enough. Perhaps this is you too. If so, just know that this is normal; *you haven't done anything wrong*. And you can fix it.

But before you can take any tactical approach to fix your business, you first need to shift your mindset. Doing the reverse doesn't work.

Why Mindset *First*, and *Then* Tactics?

It has been my experience—coaching thousands of business owners to make a bigger impact and create millions in revenue—that, before a new tactic or technique can be fully implemented and begin creating results, *the business owner's mindset has to shift.* Otherwise, the owner feels a strong resistance to actually carrying out change.

In fact, I believe (and have witnessed) that you can give any business owner a tactical solution—one that is proven to work— but if her belief systems, fears, personal rules, sense of self-worth, and self-image contradict what's required to create a shift in behavior, she will resist the tactic. Resistance creates inaction. She will stay in her current situation for years to come, or until her mindset is transformed.

Conversely, if we work on her mindset *first*, and change her beliefs or remove the fears that are getting in the way, her resistance to making necessary changes disappears almost instantaneously. That's when she will easily implement the strategy that will *see* her to success.

So, this is why, in the Leveraged Business program, we always start with shifting the mindset *first*, before getting into the nitty-gritty how-tos of strategy.

After more than twenty years of experience, I know that 95 percent of transformation starts in the mindset. Once this is in place, everything else follows easily.

Part of adopting an effective mindset involves shedding your previous limited thinking. (No judgment here; I too continually have to shed old mindsets and beliefs to be able to move to my next level.)

Scaling your business to multiple Six Figures or even a million or more requires that you embrace *a new way of thinking and acting*. This sometimes means you have to shift from being a people pleaser, and following old rules about not taking up too much space, to breaking those outdated paradigms and becoming a bigger version of yourself, more courageous and bolder.

It may mean seeking out help instead of remaining a lone ranger who prides herself on figuring things out on her own, come hell or high water.

What Makes This Book Different from Other Business Books

This is not your typical business book, dispensing advice on strategy that's difficult to apply. While it will cover many tactics and proven techniques, it is grounded in psychology. It covers the *mindset* required for scaling your business and adding a zero to your revenues, as you regain balance in your personal life.

It is likely that, as you read this book, you will feel confronted, as some of your long-standing beliefs are challenged. At the same time, you may be inspired to approach your business in a completely different way.

This is exactly what mindset is about: *the balance between beneficial confrontation and inspiration.*

Admittedly, working on your mindset can be challenging. Throughout these pages, you may experience a little tough love. This is me pushing you to be the version of you that you can't see for yourself yet. But make no mistake—my tough love places an emphasis on *love*. In fact, what makes our program different is that everything we do starts and ends with *authenticity, integrity*, and *love*.

In the program, we love fiercely. We believe in you more than you may believe in yourself. And at the same time—our members know this about me—*I'm loving, but not lenient*. Which means that, in these pages, I will always lovingly ask you to dig a little deeper.

I want to show you what you're capable of and to activate this potential for greatness, both in your business and in service to the legions of people who are waiting to work with you and your company. And I want to open up the potential of your personal life too—stretching your vision for how good your life can be.

I am taking a stand for you and for your bright future, with love and compassion. I believe in you and what you're capable of achieving.

What most of us business owners need (and secretly wish for, even when we're rugged individualists) is trusted advice. We yearn for a road map to tell us what to do next and exactly how to do it. We want guidance from people who have successfully overcome what we're dealing with, who are on the other side of this frustration point, actually enjoying entrepreneurship.

The proven mindset principles in this book are drawn from over twenty years of work with tens of thousands of customers and clients in our programs. This book will guide you to the *mindset you need to grow your business*. Once the mindset is established, the Leveraged Business program can show you exactly *how to make those changes.*

We business owners want to spend time with people who won't think we're crazy—people who understand our problems intimately. People who can provide a solution to the frustrations we're feeling. Remember: you are far from alone.

If You're Not Yet at Six Figures in Your Business

If you haven't yet reached 100K a year or a minimum of 8K a month in your business, some of these principles may not feel applicable. If that's the case, there's lots for you to explore on our other website, www.Boldheart.com. There you will find other free resources (and programs) to help you get more clients and make more money. Once you've applied these strategies and reached Six Figures, you'll be at the Leverage stage, and will gain much more from the discussion within these pages.

Introduction

"A strong focus now creates a different future later."

—Fabienne Fredrickson

I T WAS in New York City, circa 2004, that I cried on the phone with a friend. We were talking about life purpose and I remember sharing with her how deeply I wanted to know my purpose and use my business as a way of bringing my calling into the world. As she patiently listened, I remember her telling me that the way to find out my life purpose starts with focusing on the things that I am passionate about, and that the clues were there if I listened hard enough to my heart.

Even though I had no idea at the time where that would lead me, I vowed to follow the breadcrumbs of the things that made me feel alive, and to steer my business in that direction. I knew that I wanted to change people's lives with my knowledge and my expertise, but I wasn't sure 1) how to do that, and 2) how to do it in a big way.

At the time, I was a few years into running my own coaching business showing heart-centered solo entrepreneurs, experts, coaches, and consultants how to get more clients. I was becoming known for The Client Attraction System® that I'd invented and, over time, realized that my best clients were the ones who had a message to share. They had big hearts and they wanted to change people's lives. Some even wanted to change the world in their own way. So I showed them how to do so, as well as how to make very good money doing their work in the world.

I seemed to be good at this, based on the clients' results, and as I began to uncover my life's purpose and weave it into my work, my business rapidly grew to Six Figures. I was thrilled with the growth of the financial side of the business (my revenues began to match the Wall Street salary of my husband, Derek), but at the same time, I was getting more and more overwhelmed keeping up with all the work.

Derek and I had had a longtime tradition. Every now and then, I would call him at work to tell him that I had signed on a new client that day, and we would celebrate that night with a glass of champagne. But one day, I called him to let him know that I had signed on another new client and instead of him congratulating me, there was hesitation in his voice. And then silence on the line.

I said, "What's wrong?" and he gently asked me if I could really handle so many clients. He had always been a consistent supporter of my dreams and goals, and yet he reminded me that I was already at full capacity, and my practice was bursting at the seams with more than thirty clients. He quietly mentioned that he and my young daughter Claire didn't get to see me that much anymore. I was working evenings and part of the weekend, not always sleeping through the night because I had so much on my mind, and trying to keep it all together.

My eyes welled with tears because I knew he was right. I was stretched very thin, but I was also conflicted. Part of me knew that because of the way I was running my business, I was overwhelmed. The conflict was that, deep down, I knew that I wanted to grow further, to help so many more people achieve more in their business, and yet I just didn't know how to grow my own business without creating more problems and sinking deeper into overwhelm.

I saw colleagues of mine making 50K a month, I'd heard of millionaire entrepreneurs, but truth be told, I didn't see it as a reality for me. I felt small, inadequate—and that, perhaps, I wasn't good enough to make that kind of an impact and attract that kind of money.

Beyond how I saw myself and my abilities, I also just didn't know what I didn't know about growing and scaling a newly minted six-figure business so that I could work with many more clients at the same time, while getting my life back. It seemed almost impossible to have both, and I honestly didn't see the light at the end of the tunnel. That is . . .

. . . until I worked on my mindset.

In my quest for taking my business to a much higher level, I had begun to delve into lots of personal-growth and spiritual-development books, programs, and coaching. I worked with intuitive healers, Emotional Freedom Technique (EFT) practitioners, and hypnosis, all to help me move past my limiting beliefs and get out of my own way so that I could achieve more in my business and improve my quality of life. Working on my mindset, alongside my business growth activities, became my focus.

I realized that my existing beliefs were creating my current reality. At the time, I believed that more clients brought more problems. As I changed my beliefs, my mindset shifted and I began dreaming bigger, taking bolder actions, and creating unprecedented results that surprised me. All the steps I took with my mindset helped me leverage different parts of my business and scale it to a million in revenue in 2008, and then multiply that over time.

Yes, I grew this initial company, Client Attraction (now called Boldheart, the parent company to our many different brands) from thirty clients to more than three hundred active members and thousands of customers each year, but I also grew my freedom. The more I challenged my existing beliefs and ways of doing things, my vacation days multiplied.

The more I increased my sense of self-worth, the more I was able to attract and keep a team of uniquely talented people who were happy to work on the things I didn't know how to do, didn't enjoy doing, or didn't have time to do—and this freed me up to focus on a strategy for increased growth, while simultaneously spending more time with my husband and my children, of which there are now three.

Just to put the power of mindset work in perspective for you, over a period of three years, my business grew 543 percent, and *Inc.* magazine named it one of America's Fastest-Growing Private Companies three years in a row. Revenues soared, I was well supported, and we were changing lives by showing our business growth and Leverage process to other experts, coaches, consultants, thought leaders, speakers, and solo entrepreneurs. And yet, I was no longer working evenings and weekends, and was able to take a full month off here or there.

That's when I realized that I was onto something.

When I asked myself how, specifically, I had been able to do this, I reverse engineered my journey and figured out that I had used Eight Levers to scale the business in record time. It really was a simple process, and the following image came to mind:

Imagine eight light switches on the wall of a dark room.

Imagine now flipping one of the light switches, and the room getting a little brighter. This is what happens when you use one of the Eight Leveraged Business Activators you will read about in these pages. You are less in the dark, and things get clearer.

Each time you flip another light switch (another Leverage Activator), the room gets significantly brighter, and things are clearer. And when you have flipped all eight light switches, the room is fully bright and you can see everything clearly. Quite a difference from not seeing the light at the end of the tunnel.

In translating this to your own business, it means that as you fully implement the Eight Leveraged Business Activators, you will go from being overwhelmed at Six Figures, to reaching Seven Figures while getting your life back. It is a truly magical result, and yet it's also predictable when you apply the process. The Leverage process has worked for more than four hundred business owners at the time of writing this book, and they saw results anywhere from doubling to quadrupling their revenues. It has taken as little as a year for a member of our program to reach Seven Figures, although in our experience, the average has been three to five years. The timing depended on how far along owners were in their businesses, and how quickly they implemented the program.

This is the process I've included in this book: the one that my Team of coaches and I teach in the Leveraged Business program (**www.TheLeveragedBusiness.com**)

But this is not about me, my Team, past members or our program. It's about you.

You might remember that I began this introduction talking about life's purpose. This very much ties in to the Leverage process. Here's what I mean.

I now believe deep in my heart that the things we are passionate about are not random—they are our calling. Once we're clear on why we're here, I believe that shifting our mindset is the key to amplifying our work in the world to really make a difference in people's lives and for the greater whole (and, of course, to be handsomely rewarded for it).

Why is this relevant to scaling your business? Well, you likely started your business because you are passionate about something, or you want to create a change or help a certain type of individual. And my belief is that you aren't here to work with just ten to twenty clients each year. No, you were meant for more impact.

You see, I believe that all human beings have a song to sing that only they can sing, and that this song needs to be heard far and wide. Problem is, the mindset of most business owners keeps their reach small. What stops them from singing their song at a higher volume? The belief that having a big impact isn't for them, that they are small, that they don't have what it takes to get their message or service out there to a much larger audience. They also don't fully see that it is absolutely possible to achieve a much higher quality of life while doing so.

This Leverage process is about stretching your capacity for working with many more clients and customers, and creating a much bigger impact in the world as a result of shifting how you do your business. It is a predictable process, a recipe of sorts. Follow it and see your impact grow.

In the end, I'd like you to remember this:

Over the last 13.7 billion years, there has never been anyone like you. There is no one like you now, and there will never ever be anyone like you again. That calling, that song that is yours to sing, and your business simply need to be leveraged. I am delighted to help you do this.

I believe in you and in your mission.

Thank you for trusting me on this journey.

We're here if you need us to help you implement it.

Love,

P.S. The light at the end of the tunnel is now galloping toward you.

THE
LEVERAGED
Business

Leverage Your Team

OBJECTIVE:

Learn how to hire great people you trust who will take everything off your plate so you can focus on exponential growth.

I HAVE LONG believed that being a business owner means making a difference in people's lives—sometimes just in our immediate communities; sometimes even across the world. We have the power to irrevocably change the lives of every client or customer we touch when we work with them. By working with even more clients and customers, we can create a ripple effect in the world, even a tiny part of it.

The greater the impact we want to make through our business, the higher the level of world-class support we will require to do so.

That said, even if you don't think of your work as changing lives every day, it is important. You are here to serve people and to make a difference. And you deserve to be supported by the highest-quality people, without exception. That said, most of us were never taught how to hire world-class talent, train them, keep them, and delegate to them effectively. For most of us, the hiring process is far from strategic.

Not getting the support you *really* need, not hiring soon enough, not hiring the right people, not paying well enough, and not delegating properly or enough are all unconscious acts of *self-sabotage*. Conversely, hiring properly is an act of self-care. Surrounding yourself with the best team available is self-worth in action.

I have shouted it from the rooftops for many years: *You deserve the highest-quality support possible.*

You are worth it, your clients and customers are worth it, your mission is worth it, and you deserve to have a team of people who are uniquely brilliant in doing their work, so that you can focus on your unique brilliance as well.

Believe in yourself enough to insist on hiring only the very best people, even if it takes a little longer to find them. This is true leverage.

> **1. What got you *here* is not going to get you *there*; to grow, you must actually work *less*.**

The Control Enthusiast within is blocking your growth. When you first began your business, it was necessary for you to do everything yourself, put in long hours, and be a Control Enthusiast (a term I much prefer over the more common "Control Freak"). Good thing you did, because that is exactly what helped you bring your business to where it is today, at Six or even Seven Figures.

The problem is, you've now reached a crucial impasse that happens in every growing business: the point at which there is no more "you" to go around and no more time to work on the projects necessary to grow your business further.

You have officially become the bottleneck in your business, the one likely slowing everything down, growth and revenues included.

Because of this, the business is stuck at its current level. You're working more hours than you ever would find acceptable working for someone else, and you're likely making less personally than you would if you were to work for someone else. In fact, you're tapped out and on the way to burnout if something doesn't change soon.

If your company is not growing consistently it's because you're probably still too much in the day-to-day operations, working "in" the business, rather than "on" growing the business.

Even if you already have an established team or a part-time person in place to help you, the all-too-common mindset of *"I can do it better," "I can do it faster,"* and *"It would take me longer to train someone else to do this rather than doing it myself,"* as well as *"Why should I pay someone else to do something I can do so easily?,"* all perpetuate your position as the bottleneck of the company.

This is the Control Enthusiast position, in which absolutely everything has to be touched by you in one way or another before it goes "out there."

Now, I'm not suggesting you stop focusing on quality control, no. But the longer you stay in the role of the bottleneck in the company, having everything be done by *you* or go through *you,* the longer you will struggle and perpetuate inadequate growth.

You must now embrace your true role in the company. Instead of dealing with the day-to-day administrative tasks of your business, or being the one who delivers *all* of the work to your clients and customers, it's time for you to transition to a role in which you focus your tasks on scaling the business beyond its current iteration.

Your job as business owner must now morph to the role of the Visionary, the true entrepreneur, rather than the Doer. Instead of being the one who is locked into the day-to-day, the person who delivers the service or makes the product, going forward, you will switch to being accountable for the:

1. big future vision
2. strategy for exponential growth
3. big-picture business development
4. positioning in the marketplace
5. internal culture

When you transition from working completely IN the business (daily operations, the delivery of the entirety of goods and services, administrative work, etc.) to working more and more ON the business (mapping out exponential growth plans, overseeing the creation of scalable processes, setting up a team you trust, large-scale business development, etc.), that's when you will multiply your company's earnings, gain control of your time, and experience freedom again.

I am not sure there is such a thing as a true self-made millionaire.

To achieve more with your business, you must now get more help, expand your team even further and hire rock stars to do what you're currently doing now. This may *seem* impossible from where you're currently standing, and yet this is the rite of passage every business owner must go through to exponentially scale his or her business to its next level.

2. You deserve to (and can absolutely) hire rock stars.

You do not have "The Employee Curse"; just learn to hire better.
It can be very tempting to say, *"Okay, if the only way to achieve the next level is to hire someone, then I'll do it,"* only to go hire a friend or someone you can easily afford. You may have hired others before, only to be supremely disappointed and disillusioned that it didn't work out or that it wasn't worth the time and financial investment.

The likelihood is, you hired the wrong person.

Have some compassion for yourself, though. This happens to most business owners, especially in the beginning. Getting a person, *any person with a pulse*, to help you in the business is better than not having anyone. Or at least that's the mindset that drives people making their first hires (this happened to me too, so no judgment here). Sadly, it is a tactic devoid of strategy, one that I too practiced all too often in the beginning.

Most every time you hire someone in haste, just to *stop the bleeding*, you eventually begin to wonder why things aren't getting done, why they're getting done wrong, why mistakes are being made, and why certain aspects of that person's job are being avoided.

So you fire the person and hire the next person right under your nose, as quickly as you can, because you like them or they *seem* to know what they're doing, and, sadly, you likely experience the same disappointments all over again.

Logically, this could make you believe, especially when this happens repeatedly, that you're a terrible manager and that maybe you have the "employee curse." This curse is made up of beliefs that you are not able to hire well, keep employees, or, perhaps, that you're not meant to have any.

Worse, if this continues, you may actually contemplate not staying in business because you're stuck between a rock and a hard place: the rock is knowing that you're already overwhelmed and can't do it alone; the hard place is that you clearly can't manage other people and don't see the light at the end of this tunnel of complexity.

Which means that you stop hiring people or choose to do it by yourself, which of course doesn't work either. After many iterations, the business stops growing because you spend more time figuring out your team issues than you do scaling the business and increasing cash flow and profits.

This won't work, certainly not in the long term.

The point is, none of your assumptions about being a bad manager are correct.

No, you are not a bad manager. You simply were never taught how to hire strategically, or follow processes that bring you the right person for a particular job. You may have never been given best practices on how to delegate in a way that things get done on time, and the way you want them done.

However, when you follow a precise hiring and training methodology (more on this in a minute), everything changes. Your company then becomes a sought-out company to work for and turnover reduces drastically.

Don't hire a warm body just to stop the bleeding. Here's what's important for you to know: When you hire someone not *suited* or *wired* to do a particular type of work, they will 1) never be good at it, 2) begin resenting that part of their job, 3) likely sabotage their own efforts, and 4) may eventually leave, or force you to fire them.

Why? Because of the lack of "fit," this person's job feels to them like they are continually rowing upstream, like they are going against the grain. It's just too hard for them to do their job and you become increasingly frustrated that things aren't working out.

Hiring without strategy doesn't work. Instead, every role in your company needs someone specifically *wired* for it.

Is the position one that requires precision, specificity and exactness? Then the person you must hire for this position is someone who is process-driven, who can create systems and make sure that no one deviates from the system.

Conversely, are you looking for someone who can charm, woo and sell like nobody's business? Then this will require someone who can improvise, influence, be relationship-driven, who is unafraid of confrontation and enjoys answering objections and asking for the sale. Someone who can be pleasantly persistent.

In my experience, these two types of hires are *polar opposites.*

That said, business owners often make the mistake of trying to plug two "holes" in their company with one "stopper," thinking it's a wise move to try to hire one person for two roles, with an eye toward saving money. For example, they'll hire one person to do a combination of administrative tasks *and* sales, because they feel that there may not be enough work for a full time admin and a full time salesperson. (It's normal. I too made this mistake in the beginning.)

What the business owner doesn't realize is that they are dooming their business by making this decision. A person who loves sales typically resists minutiae, rigid processes, procedures and systems (not always, but this is often the case). They love the game of winning others over, to hunt and get things done their way, even if it doesn't follow a specific process. Often, the ends justify the means in this situation.

Conversely, a person who is wired for processes, procedures and systems, who loves dotting the "i"s and crossing the "t"s, often feels nervous when put in a position of having to improvise for too long or be quick on their feet. Often, they have a great fear of getting on the phone to ask for the business or not take no for an answer. They prefer to be behind their computer, and just get their work done, without having to interact with a lot of people. There are exceptions to this, of course, but in my experience, they are few and far between.

Where you may have previously been stuck in building your team, as I was, is in not realizing that different people are wired *differently* and should be hired accordingly.

We know this to be true because of years of seeing the proof in the pudding. Within our work, we have used several different assessments with our members over the years, and it's proven that there are different types of people with different innate skill sets, falling into distinct categories.

Some people are great at systemizing and double-checking everything, while others are more fluid and can adapt to change very quickly. Some don't mind risk and uncertainty, while their counterparts wish to stabilize every situation to reduce risk, at all cost. Some like to imagine and think conceptually, while others prefer building with their hands or seeing things detailed on paper. Finally, some like to fact-find extensively before making any decision, while others are better at going with the flow, simplifying big concepts and preferring estimations or summaries to long lists of facts.

This is important for you to know, especially if you've been unhappy with past hires. In fact, I believe there are four important components to consider when hiring someone:

1) **Skill set** (do they know how to do what you need?)
2) **Experience on the job** (how many years have they been doing it?)
3) **Culture fit** (do they have the right personality and values to get along with the other team members? Are they a natural extension of your brand?)
4) **Wiring** (are they innately wired to do the job well? Were they *born this way*?)

I now believe that the first two can be taught or eventually acquired. The second two cannot, especially the "wiring" part. I consider the wiring criteria to be the most important and weigh it accordingly in the hiring process.

To build a highly cohesive team and leverage the skills of all your team members, all must be working within their unique wiring. It's important that you know how they are specifically wired and what type of position they will thrive in. When a team member is hired for a position that uses their strengths, they produce better results, and are more productive and much happier.

This is why when hiring any new member of a team, I recommend you first look at how the candidate is wired to take action, what their innate strengths are, and how they respond to external expectations by using a variety of assessments, such as the Kolbe A Index, Gallup's StrengthsFinder tools, the Four Tendencies assessment, and others.

Using assessments with prospective team members gives you a more complete picture of whether the person in front of you will be a rock star at their particular role, or just another warm body that eventually disappoints you. This produces much better hires than hiring blindly or based on personality and past experience alone.

In our business, we follow a very specific process for using assessments and look at the results of these *before* any formal interview is ever scheduled, seeing it as the first important factor to bringing on an ideal team member. It turns the hiring process into a science rather than a game of eeny meeny miny moe.

Let me give you an example. Years ago, my Team had narrowed down the search process to one candidate for a website coding position. A meeting was scheduled for me to interview him and the day before the interview, I reviewed his assessment scores. I knew that someone for this kind of position would need to be process-driven, detail-oriented and systems-focused.

The problem is, his scores pointed entirely in the opposite direction. He was wired as someone who was erratic in this behavior, who improvised greatly, and took risks and chances. He was innately wired as the kind of person to not follow rules or processes. He had characteristics of a serial entrepreneur, someone unlikely to stick with one thing for any length of time.

These were big red flags for me, and when I gently pointed this out to the members of the team that had suggested that we hire him, they too agreed that doing so would have been a big mistake, as this was the exact opposite of the person we were looking to hire.

Yes, his skill set was good, as was his experience. But it was clear that he wouldn't have lasted long in the position and would have likely made sloppy mistakes, neither of which we were willing to experience or take a chance with. To me, it was clear that there was no reason to follow through with the interview, so we canceled it.

We ended up hiring someone perfectly wired for the position, with the right skill set, the right experience and who fit our culture perfectly. He, in turn, has been with us for many, many years and has produced exceptional work. This is an employee we consider to be a rock star. And his assessment scores (practically) predicted this.

The point I'm trying to make is the following: when you consistently hire the right team members, you build a team of uniquely brilliant people, where each person is in the right role, is wired for their role, and happy in their position. Because they love their job, they're committed to the company and stay longer, getting better and better at their role every day. They appreciate working with you and it shows.

In the end, team members who are hired properly and are a great fit for the role are more invested and productive, and feel a sense of ownership, which makes them eager to want to help move the business forward.

Having a team full of these types of hires is one element that helps you scale your business much more quickly and consistently. This is what you want.

---

3. Take the leap of faith and hire for where you're going, not for where you are now.

"I skate to where the puck is going to be, not where it has been."

—Wayne Gretzky

Yes, you *can* afford that next employee now, not later. While you likely started your business on a shoestring budget, like I did, previously having focused on low-cost to no-cost growth measures, this changes at the Leverage stage of your business. At this point, you're going to need to invest more significantly in the business and this includes investing in your team, even if it doesn't always feel like you have the cash flow to do so. I've rarely met someone at Six Figures who says, *"I have all the money in the world to hire the team I want."*

Repeatedly, business owners tell me, *"Yes, Fabienne, I dream of hiring lots of people, but I just don't have the cash to do that right now. I need to wait until the money shows up."*

Yes, admittedly, *growth sucks cash.* And that means that you don't always feel comfortable investing in your business in the form of new hires. Doing so feels like a heavy responsibility. That being said, to get to the next level of growth, and really leverage your business (eventually to Seven Figures) you will need to hire someone else to help you get out from the day-to-day operations of your business, including the administrative ones, so that you can focus on bigger projects that will help you move the company forward.

In hiring at this stage, it's tempting to want to save money and either not hire anyone until you *really* need them, hire a part-time person to save some cash, or hire someone you would score a 4 out of 10 (10 being ideal) just to save a few bucks. Instead of hiring the person you *truly* need, the one who has all four criteria to get you to that elusive next level, it's tempting to play safe and not spend the money.

The problem is, hiring inadequately is probably more detrimental to your business than investing in a great hire would be.

I've been there. There have been many times in my own business that, to move to the next big level, I had to confront a fear stemming from the following question, *"How will I be able to afford this person and everything else I need to pay for?"* Each time, the fear stopped me in my tracks. Little did I know that I wasn't the only one who experiences these fears. It's rather normal at this stage.

There are many fears that show up when it's time to hire some-one for the first time or greatly expand an existing team. Here is a list that usually resonates with our members when asked about the fears or reasons they haven't delegated or hired yet:

- *"It didn't happen the way I wanted it to so I took the work back."*
- *"It's not the right time to hire now."*
- *"I can't afford it right now."*
- *"I don't trust others to do it the way I do it."*
- *"I don't know who to hire, what their role would be, or what they would do for me."*
- *"If I hire, I might grow too big!"*
- *"It will cut into my profits."*
- *"I already have too many expenses."*
- *"I worry about all the legal, financial and tax implications of hiring."*
- *"My parents believed in the Old World work ethic and did it all themselves. They will think I'm being lazy if I don't do it myself."*
- *"Who do I think I am?"*
- *"What if they do it better than me?"*
- *"There is no one good to hire where I live."*
- *"What if my vision fails? I will feel responsible for them and their families."*
- *"What if they steal my clients or knowledge?"*
- *"I'm afraid to make a bad hire so I prefer to not hire anyone."*
- *"It's comfortable this way."*
- *"It means more people to manage!"*
- *"It's just easier to do it myself."*
- *"Not many people know how to do what I do."*

- *"Hiring another person will rock the boat with my existing team."*
- *"It will be painful and time consuming to train someone else."*
- *"I fear they won't service my clients like I do."*
- *"Hiring someone to replace my role is not common in my industry."*
- *"I don't want to feel responsible or accountable to others."*
- *"I can afford one person but I need two. I'm paralyzed with not knowing who to hire first and I don't know where to start."*
- *"I feel guilty that they will do the work and I'll have less to do. What will I do with all my free time?"*
- *"What if I hired them and they then leave me!"*
- *"What if I lose my sense of boundaries and overgive?"*
- *"What if I hurt people's feelings in the process?"*
- *"What if my clients leave because they're no longer working directly with me?"*
- *"I don't want to get too big and feel too corporate!"*
- *"It will be more work for me."*
- *"I'll feel overly responsible for the well-being of others."*
- *"I don't like to manage people and I'm not good at HR."*
- *"What if it doesn't make me more money?"*
- *"It would mean getting an office and that would cost me more money."*
- *"I don't have space in my office and I don't want to manage people remotely."*
- *"I'm afraid of losing time and money if the hire doesn't work out or doesn't do the work right."*
- *"I'm scared I'll spend all my time managing people instead of doing my work!"*

Do you recognize some of your own mindset blocks on this list? (If so, it's absolutely normal at this stage of your business.)

It's a common dance among growth-minded entrepreneurs, a dance called *resistance*. You feel that you're "too big to be small and continue doing everything yourself" while at the same time being "too small to hire big." Again, this is commonplace and also a rite of passage for getting to the other side of exponential growth.

Because of the doubt and fear that come up with hiring, it's tempting to think about shooting for a "safe" option: hiring someone part-time or who is less than adequate because you want to save money; you're too scared to commit a full time employee or someone you consider to be in the "big leagues."

Here's what I see people do: they need an operations manager to take over the day-to-day operations of the business, but they get really nervous about paying this type of yearly salary, so they say, *"I'll just look for a part-time administrative person to do that job."* The problem with doing this is that a part-time assistant is typically a person who will never be as invested as a full-time team member would. They typically just don't yet have the gravitas to run the day-to-day operations of what will become a million-dollar (or million-pound) company. In my observation, there is often a different mindset in someone part-time from someone who has committed to a full-time career.

If you have hired someone, but not someone you feel great about, you've essentially bluffed yourself into thinking that you successfully took care of the problem, but in fact, you didn't. Deep inside, you still feel the need to micromanage, to double check everything and you may even feel that the proverbial "other shoe" will soon drop.

Yes, you saved a few bucks, but you also likely became (or will continue to be) the bottleneck in your company. Even with this hire, there will still not be enough of you to go around, not enough time to get everything done, and things will continue to stay at the status quo, leaving you wondering why you even bothered to hire anyone in the first place.

This may inevitably lead you to think, *"See, I knew it! I hired someone and, as always, it didn't work! It wasn't worth the time to train them or the money I spent. I'm still overwhelmed and I don't feel I've gotten ahead. Now I have to let this person go, and as always, I'm alone again and back to square one."*

When hired properly, each one of your employees will pay for themselves. Listen, I get it. Right now, cash is likely tight and you're not sure whether you can afford the person you *really* need. But without better support in the business, you will probably continue to stay stuck and overwhelmed.

What do you do? Here's a six-step "Hire Hustle" process we teach in the program that shifts your mindset and your ability to hire now, not later:

1) **Get clarity on who you really need now**: Imagine that your business is at "full practice capacity" or that you can already afford hiring someone key. Who would you hire?

2) **Do your due diligence**: Assess the risks by asking yourself: *"What will happen if I do hire this person? What will happen if I don't? What won't happen if I hire this person? What won't happen if I don't hire this person?"* If it becomes clear that the opportunity cost of staying with your current level of team support is too great, then it is likely time to hire.

3) **Evaluate the situation strategically:** Ask yourself what sort of cash flow would have you afford this person now, rather than later. *"How many more clients or customers do I need to attract per month to pay for this person?"*

4) **Increase your marketing and sales efforts** to attract and sign on the number of new clients and customers you need per month so that you can afford the new hire.

5) **Dig deep**: Take a leap of faith and hire only the person you really need, not a person you would rate a 5 out of 10.

6) **Be strategic about the first projects you give them:** Put your new hire on tasks or projects that allow them to pay for

themselves, whether these are directly revenue-generating, taking vast numbers of things off your plate so you can focus on money-generating activities, or simply creating systems or processes that allow the business to serve more people without you spending the time doing more work.

Instead of seeing the act of hiring someone new as a *cost*, using this process allows you to see this new hire as someone who *pays for him or herself.*

From my experience, if you've hired the right person, and you train them properly, focusing on a quick return on monthly investment, they will often pay for themselves in as little as three to four months.

The additional benefit of having a full-time person who is really suited to help you is that you're much more likely to start *delegating* things instead of staying in a place of overwhelm and *white knuckling* from a place of control. You will likely find yourself saying, *"Well, I'm paying for that operations manager or assistant, and he's not as busy as I'd like him to be. I might as well offload all of this other stuff to him!"*

The result of boldly hiring someone new using this process is that it frees you up to work on important growth tasks that you would never have been able to focus on otherwise. At the same time, the amount of implementation and action overall in the business increases rapidly, which drives growth and revenues forward without you being the one to do all of the driving.

4. Drive-by delegating is crippling your business.

In the realm of delegation, your employees likely aren't the problem as much as you are. Congratulations! You got clear on your hiring needs and how the person should be wired to succeed in that role; you did your due diligence; you evaluated how many more clients you would need to pay for your new hire and increased sales and marketing efforts; then you strategically came up with things for this person to do so that they would pay for themselves. You did the hardest part.

Or did you?

With a new hire in place, when it comes time to delegate, many business owners assume that this person will just *know* intuitively what to do, what it's supposed to look like, how to get it done, and when it is due for completion, like you would.

The problem with this theory is that you're not "most people."

You are an individualist.

You had the courage to leave the herd and start your own business. In the beginning, you did everything yourself, without anyone's help (you had no choice as you had no cash). Very often, you acted intuitively and impulsively. You know what it's like to be the lone ranger who is comfortable figuring it out on your own, without much help from anyone.

And, by God, you expect the people you hire to do the same, and be able to figure it out on their own, too! I mean, that's why you hired them, right? You can almost hear yourself say, *"That's right! They should know intuitively what to do without me holding their hand. Isn't that what I'm paying them so much money for??"*

This is what I affectionately call *Drive-by Delegating*: where you are so relieved to finally have help that you cocoon into your office and get on with your work without checking in with your new hire much. Or, you assume your new team member should know what's expected of them and should go off to do it on their own, without much input or direction from you.

If either of these scenarios is the approach you've taken in the past, the result is going to be a less-than-ideal outcome of disappointment and frustration, on both sides.

Business owners who take this approach very quickly get angry, saying, *"Three weeks into this and it's not even done right?? What have they been doing all this time? I could have done it myself in just three days, and it would have been so much better!"*

Disappointed and frustrated, the business owner fires the employee or independent contractor. Then hires another one. The same process occurs, the same result, and then the same outcome, again and again. And the business owner begins to question if she'll ever be able to manage people or whether this is ever going to work.

"See, I told you I was a bad manager! I knew this wouldn't work!"

But, it doesn't have to be this way.

The mindset shift required to turn this around is to realize that (in most cases) nothing was wrong with the employee. No, the problem lies in *drive-by delegating.* And the responsibility to get the right outcome is yours, not theirs. (Again, have some compassion for yourself, this is absolutely normal until you are taught how to delegate differently.)

Give your team members what they need to succeed and they will. Along the way, it's easy for a team member to feel lost, frustrated and to be embarrassed about asking for more direction from you. More than anything, they want to do good work and make you proud. They don't want to bother you too much, or feel like an annoyance to you.

You must know though, that not having enough direction or guidance from you will mean they'll go down the wrong rabbit hole, one you won't find out about until the project is past due. The end result will likely not be what you wanted, not even close. You'll feel frustrated and they'll feel embarrassed.

Here's the thing: It's not the employee's job to read your mind or guess what you want her to do or what the finished project will look like. Especially if your team members are wired differently than you are, it's imperative that you give them the tools they need to produce the desired outcome, efficiently and on time.

This requires that you learn to delegate properly.

Your job going forward is to shift your mindset to equip your team members to succeed. You do this by giving them:

1) **Specificity** about what the ideal outcome should look like for it to be a success, including success criteria for the project ("for this project to be done well, it must have x, y and z elements"; give them some sketches, past examples to work from or whatever will help them visualize or be clear on what you're expecting of them).

2) **Direction** on exactly how to do it (checklists, documented processes, resources, etc.). And no, don't worry, you're not the one who will create the checklists. More on that later.

3) **A realistic deadline** that is communicated to them, rather than ASAP (first draft is due on Tuesday, second draft a week later, and the final project is due on the thirtieth).

4) **An opportunity for clarification** of what's expected of them. (*"Would you like to repeat back to me what the project should look like? Do you feel like you have enough direction? Are there questions you have for me about moving forward? What are your thoughts or concerns about this?"*)

5) **Regular access to you for questions**, every step of the way. (*"Tell me about your progress since we last met. What have you accomplished? What aspects of the project are you working on now? Where are you stuck? What's not working? How can I help?"*)

This is not about impatiently awaiting results, but rather investing in their training so that you can eventually have a self-sustaining team that feels empowered to do things without you having to micromanage them.

If you'd like to get increasingly better results from your team and avoid a revolving door of independent contractors or employees, change your mindset around how to communicate with and delegate to each team member.

Take on the role of *coach*, not dictator or wizard behind the curtain, the one they never see. This is an internal shift *you* must make, focusing on the long-term success and the future of your team and your company. Doing this empowers your team to *eventually* know how to do things without much input from you.

It's worth putting in the effort *now* and going forward, even if you have too much on your plate currently. This is what will scale your business significantly.

In the end, you owe it to yourself and your big mission to leverage a uniquely brilliant team, one made up of rock stars in different disciplines of your business (marketing, sales, operations, customer care, finance and human resources, etc.) Obviously, not every business starts needing all of these different disciplines at once. But over time and as your business grows, you will eventually hire them so you can remove yourself from these areas.

You don't need to be well-rounded, you need to be well-supported.

As I mentioned before, I have never met a self-made millionaire. The person who reaches Seven Figures is the one who is smart enough to recognize that she cannot do it alone, that she must focus on what she's exceptionally capable of doing, and that she is deserving enough to be helped by people who are capable of doing things she cannot. That's how you get to Seven Figures and gain your life and freedom back.

What's the impact of applying the Team Activator in your business? Rachel explains it to you in her own words:

"Eight years later, we've gone from one team member to eight, revenues have gone from low Six Figures to very close to Seven Figures, and we are leaders in our field. My mindset is supported here at the Leveraged Business program in a way that allows me to lead this company and handle anything that comes my way. The community is amazing. Everyone is each other's champion.

"So yes, when my well-meaning team member asked me (back in 2009) whether the program was really worth it and whether we couldn't simply figure this out on our own . . . Yes, it's worth it. I wouldn't be where I am without Fabienne and the community I have found in this program.

"If you're ready to have an amazing home to grow yourself and your business, there's nothing else out there quite like this." — Rachel Wall

Leverage Your
Systems

OBJECTIVE:

Create structure and control in your business through documented processes, so everything runs smoothly and no longer requires your daily involvement.

L ET'S FACE IT. You likely started your business by being a risk-taker, doing things when they needed to get done (even if they weren't perfect) and not necessarily following any rules or documented path. It was a highly intuitive process because there was simply too much to do at the time and you did what you could to fix problems and get to the solution as quickly as possible.

Because of this, if we're being honest, sometimes your business looks like it is being held together by toothpicks and Band-Aids— disparate pieces thrown together without rhyme or reason. And yes, that worked for a long time. After all, it was just you in the beginning and that's about as much as you could manage without falling apart. Your go-to command was probably, *"All hands on deck! I'll do what I can to stop the chaos, but then, I need to move on to important things."*

The problem is, the exponential growth of a business doesn't happen when it's built upon a house of cards being held together with very little glue.

To scale your business (and income) to its next level, and for you to get your life back and have things run smoothly with or without you, this must now change. You can no longer afford to run your business by the seat of your pants. You must now leverage systems for everything, absolutely everything. Don't worry, it's not difficult when you are shown how.

---

1. Although it feels counterintuitive, systems liberate you and give you the freedom you seek.

You've resisted predictability and structure, but now it's time to embrace these like never before. The mindset of an overwhelmed business owner is often tied to this idea of being a rugged individualist who doesn't have to answer to anyone and does what he or she wants.

You pride yourself on being an individual who can do things on your own, who can make it up as you go. You've shied away from too many rules and restrictions in your life because they typically feel suffocating to you. Besides, you likely don't think in terms of processes as much as you like to create shortcuts, change direction when needed, be flexible and find ways around problems on your own.

The issue is that all of this requires an enormous amount of energy and lots of time, neither of which you have enough of in your current stage of business. You are likely exhausted. This is the biggest reason you are not growing. The longer you keep operating this way, the more complexity and chaos you will add to the business, delaying growth and any feeling of freedom.

You can't be in the weeds and planting the garden at the same time.

As your business heads into its next growth phase, you will need to begin embracing the idea of having systems, something you have likely resisted. Having structure and a set of processes will give you your time back, drastically reduce or eliminate headaches, liberate you and increase your revenues and profits, while giving you the freedom and predictable growth you seek.

At this stage of business, it will be very different to grow without having systems in place. There's no way around it.

With the right systems in place and everyone following them (including you), *you* are no longer needed to put out fires. Imagine what would happen if everything in your business was predictable, in a good way. Imagine that you are no longer required to handle the details of your business; imagine that things consistently get done on time, on budget and within a certain set of desired specifications.

How would that feel? How would that make a difference in your life?

You see, when everything is documented and systematized, and your processes are consistently improved, your role in the business shifts dramatically. Issues either 1) don't come up, 2) take care of themselves, or 3) get handled by a team member, which means you have more time to be strategic about the big picture and time off to enjoy your life again.

When things no longer fall through the cracks, chaos is removed, the day-to-day operations of the business no longer require you to be involved and you can begin shifting your role in the company from a reactive stance to a proactive leadership role.

This requires a shift in self-image from being *the person who delivers the work and drives every aspect of the business* to a self-image rooted in being *the passive investor with a reduced daily involvement in the business, happily collecting a check.*

What a difference in identity!

---

2. Your mindset must now embrace you as the leader of a process-driven company.

A person-assembled business is impossible to scale. When I first hired team members, I picked personalities I liked or created positions around people I knew. I would ask, *"What are you good at? What can you do? Okay, cool, I like you. You're hired!"* and then scramble to find something for them to do in my business, based on who they were, not necessarily what I needed most at that time.

Without realizing it, I was creating a team based on the people immediately under my nose, rather than the roles I desperately needed to fill to move my business forward. I've encountered this countless times in the many hundreds of six-figure businesses we've mentored.

The business owner assembles a hodge-podge of people, hoping it will all work out and that the people will stay. Problem is, personalities are not always predictable. People change, people leave and there is too much room for human error.

Consistency comes from stability, regularity, dependability, reliability, and uniformity, which are ultimately what scales a business. These exist in a business that runs on systems, processes and operations. Reliability is the opposite of how most businesses start out. Conversely, consistency positions your business to run like a well-oiled cash machine that doesn't require you to be there day-in and day-out.

Dependability can even position your business to be sold for millions down the line.

Why? Because a process-driven business can be scaled and successfully replicated again and again. This can be seen ubiquitously in franchise restaurants that are able to produce the same product in one part of the globe as in another across the world. This is because the restaurant is process-run.

It doesn't matter if the two locations have totally different owners (franchisees) who speak different languages, have different cultures and personalities. The product is predictably similar because the business is process-driven rather than people-driven.

(This doesn't mean your business will become unfeeling or unkind. The right people working in your business will *appreciate* that there are systems to follow as it eliminates chaos.)

The same process that franchises use to scale can be used in your business too. Going forward, you may wish to shift your view of your business from a personality-driven business (yours or your team's) to a scalable business model that is focused on processes, systems and operations, rather than on a set of people who cannot be duplicated exactly.

It's miraculous what happens when you're willing to do that. Every one of our members who have successfully crossed the seven-figure mark implemented this. It's simply a rite of passage, one that you'll want to participate in as well.

Consistency can be achieved when every function within your business is documented and produces predictable, verifiable results. Anything done more than once a year in your business should ideally have a system around it, preferably documented in an Operations Manual with checklists that describe several processes: "How we do things around here." This can include the HR process, the sales and marketing process, the customer service process, etc.

When every process is documented, it is no longer swimming in your head (or another key employee's head) and can be continually updated, added to and used for training new employees in a shorter period of time than you would ever be able to without it having been documented.

Now, understandably, this seems like a Herculean task, especially when you are not one who enjoys structure. For many business owners, an Operations Manual is not urgent and is more of a "nice to have" because it isn't seen as directly and immediately bringing in more money for the business. This is one of the reasons it often gets pushed to the back burner and stays there collecting dust.

That being said, shortly after the Operations Manual takes form, is put into place, and is followed by all, revenues typically go up, the owner's total number of work hours go down, productivity increases, issues are reduced, clients and customers are happier, referrals go up, and profit increases. This often results in more money and better cash flow because the owner is not as involved in the minutiae, and is now able to focus on growth.

Sounds worth it, right?

The key to running your business from an operations perspective can be revealed through a simple exercise:

I'd like for you to imagine that, in exactly one year's time, you were to be given an opportunity to go on sabbatical for a year to do something you've always wanted to do, something that requires that you remove yourself from your business entirely for one year, with the simple caveat that your business must keep going strong and profitably without you being involved for more than two to four hours a week.

The question to ask yourself is the following:

"For the business to run successfully without me, or even to be duplicated without me being there, what would need to be in place to produce similar, if not better, results?"

This is the beginning of your Operations Manual, and your freedom as well.

3. You are not the one to create or run the Operations Manual.

Yes, everything needs to be documented, but you don't have to be the one to do it—you just need to create the shell of it. When a business owner on the verge of leveraging their business hears that it's time to document every single process in her business, down to each excruciatingly small detail, a look of dread usually crosses her face.

The thought of doing something that goes against the grain is daunting, even revolting for many. Worse, she feels there's already not enough time to work on money-generating activities, let alone something like the Operations Manual that doesn't initially bring in new leads, clients, or cash.

A shift in mindset is required here.

Your job is now to *help define* the processes that must be outlined, as well as a deadline by which they must be documented. Then, it's every team member's job to document each procedure as they do it each time.

Yes, perhaps they'll grumble at first, as this seems to them to be an unnecessary process since the information lives conveniently and comfortably in their heads. To overcome the grumbling from team members, share the vision of what the company will look like when everything is process-driven, how everything will run more smoothly and efficiently for each team member.

They will write it. Instead of you, the business owner, putting a pause on driving sales, each member of your team will write their section of the Operations Manual, focusing on the big picture (process) and then small details (checklists and how-to).

Communicate to each team member the advantages of them having a well-documented Operations Manual. This can include benefits such as reduced work hours for the team member, more predictable results, fewer things falling through the cracks, a sense of pride and fulfillment, or possibly even more time off.

Listing out the benefits they will personally receive is usually enough to get them excited to work on it, especially if it's a company-wide effort and there is a common deadline by which this must be completed, perhaps even followed by a celebration or team reward.

Your systems must be run by people who are not entrepreneurial. Making sure that "t"s are crossed and "i"s are dotted *after* a system has been created is usually not the business owner's forte. Often, the person who created the system is also not the one who is wired to run it for years to come.

There are indeed people, such as project managers, who love to work on a big project and give it their all until its completion. These are also usually the same people who are excited to move on to another project and aren't interested in revisiting project A or running it.

This is where a welcome addition to the team is someone wired as a process manager or operations manager, someone who gets great satisfaction from taking a process and making sure it keeps being updated and followed by all. This process-driven person will likely not be the business owner, at least not for the long term, but someone who is happy leading, managing and holding team members accountable, and keeping projects going consistently.

The ideal process manager or operations manager is someone who likes to be exact, create a plan, design sequential systems, honor deadlines, categorize and organize things that are similar, and who prefers to have closure and order. At the same time, they like to create undeviating standards, protect the status quo, create precedents, and reduce unexpected events.

This is usually not how you, the business owner, operate, as you typically like to improvise. Having someone on your team who can specify, systematize and stabilize will provide the balance needed to map out (and run) the systems and Operations Manual that allow your business to grow further and scale to new heights.

---

4. With the right systems, you can be high-touch in a high-tech world.

Even emotion can be generated systematically. Sometimes, our members in the program are afraid to create systems and document what is done in their business because they pride themselves in special touches that are intuitive, heartfelt and customized. Yes, making clients feel special is an important part of keeping them and generating referrals, which is also an important way to leverage your business.

A gift here, a handwritten note there, or a special touch that wasn't expected can all further the relationship with a client or customer and have a very positive long-term impact.

The problem is that many business owners who do these high-touch gestures are initiating them personally. This is fine in the beginning when a business owner has ten to twenty clients, but it's not scalable when we're looking to leverage the business to have one to two hundred clients or one to two thousand ongoing customers, for example.

The feel-good actions (and resulting positive emotions the clients feel) should absolutely continue, but they too can be put into a predictable, well-thought-out process, such as automated birthday cards, that replaces the business owner's manual, time-consuming role. Or, it can be delegated, of course.

The issue is that many entrepreneurs worry that, once they stop manually initiating high-touch, feel-good actions in their business, they will lose the relationship with the clients; or that when things are overly systemized, the business will feel "cold."

This is not necessarily the case. If left to you and only you, perhaps you wouldn't make that nice gesture for those one hundred or one thousand clients, every time, simply because there are other more pressing things looming. But with a system in place, making the client feel special can become a predictable, repeatable process that never falls through the cracks, which is infinitely better than nothing at all.

This can show up as a welcome gift that is automatically generated each time a new client signs up. For example, we have sent our members a box of delicious brownies and a smiley-face sticker on a welcome kit that says, *"Please do not open this box until you've called this 1-800 number and have listened to my welcome greeting"),* or we have sent a birthday card and gift every year, one week before the customer's birthday.

Feeling good can be a systematic, orchestrated process that clients love, even if they're unclear as to whether it's part of a system or not. Despite the fact that they know you've sent them an automated card or a box of brownies in the mail upon signing with you, they are still impressed by the gesture (and respect the system) because of the loving intention behind it and the fact that no other company they deal with is likely doing as much for them as your company is.

These kinds of systems can produce raving fans and, once established, don't require any extra time or involvement from the business owner. It is a scalable process that still feels good on the receiving end.

5. Have systems in place to continually improve your systems.

Problems and mistakes are *great* for moving your company forward. Having systems and processes in place for each and every aspect of your business doesn't mean there will no longer be issues or problems that arise. There will be and you can count on that. But whereby a problem or issue could bring your business to a standstill in the past, when everything is documented and running like a well oiled machine, a new issue will only point to a part of a system that needs tweaking, and it can be handled quickly and efficiently with a "systems-improvement process."

When an issue arises or a project fails, it can actually be a blessing if you shift your mindset from "failure" to "opportunity for lasting improvement." This is your cue to look at the "mistake" as a fault in a current system, trace it back to its origin, take the lesson you learned from it, and create another system around it to better it, for good.

Here's how you do it: examine any situation, event or occurrence that originally seemed like a failure in your business and allow yourself time to process it from a strategic viewpoint.

If you've ever seen the 1993 comedy *Groundhog Day* with Bill Murray and Andie McDowell, you know that Murray plays Phil Connors, an arrogant Pittsburgh TV weatherman who, during an assignment covering the annual Groundhog Day event in Punxsutawney, Pennsylvania, finds himself waking up to the same day again and again.

Each "day" plays out exactly as the previous one, but only Phil is aware of this time loop. At first he is confused, but when the phenomenon continues on subsequent days, he decides to take advantage of the lack of long-term consequences and, for lack of a better word, abuse his privileges.

Eventually, Phil uses the time loop to his own benefit, not only to improve himself, but to gain the attention of his love interest. He begins to use his by-now vast knowledge of the day's unfolding events to help as many people around town as possible and subsequently woo McDowell's character. And it works.

Despite great initial frustration and self-sabotage, Phil embraces the situation, figures out what works about it and what doesn't, and when given the opportunity to experience the time loop of February

2 all over again, he eventually applies all his hard-earned lessons, creating new systems along the way.

He uses his past failed experiences to better his future experiences and create predictable outcomes.

This is what you want in your company: predictable outcomes.

We've named this process the *Groundhog Day exercise.* Our members use it to learn from each experience (positive or negative, internal or client-facing) so that they can improve their internal processes and create new systems for everything. Fewer things fall through the cracks, which translates to creating "problem free zones" that can be enjoyed for years to come.

Embrace the issues that arise in your business like the irritant that causes a pearl to be formed in an oyster. Our culture teaches us that problems are bad and should be avoided at all cost. But not every problem is bad, and in fact, it can actually be good for business, as long as the same problem only happens once and can be built upon to create a solid company.

Here's the analogy I'd like to share with you so that you don't feel down on yourself each time a problem arises in your business:

If you understand that pearls are formed inside the shell of an oyster as a defense mechanism against an irritant that enters its shell, you can shift your mindset around that grain of sand, the irritant. What creates a beautiful pearl is when the oyster deposits layers of calcium carbonate around the irritant.

The irritant is a necessary part of success in this case, as it initiates the creation of something beautiful. Without the irritant or problem, the pearl would not have been generated.

In the same way, an issue in your business can be just the thing to trigger a system that forever enhances your business, especially when you use a process such as the *Groundhog Day* exercise. With every system you add to your business, you make your company even more valuable, most consistent, reliable, and predictable (in a good way).

This effectively allows you to remove yourself from the day-to-day operations of the business, and have the business grow more consistently, while you gain your life back.

Problems can be viewed differently when you shift your mindset toward leverage. You don't wish for them, but when they arrive, you embrace them as an agent of positive change for the long-term health of your company.

What's the impact of applying the Systems Activator in your business? Suzanne explains it to you in her own words:

"I'm at the end of my second year in the Leveraged Business program. We were already a seven-figure business when we joined, with a tremendous reach all around the country and globally. But my concern was how do we continue the legacy and how do we make this successful for another thirty-five years?

"So, my sister and I actually joined together. At the time, I spent 60 percent of my time traveling even though I have three children at home. I was burnt out. I love what I do. I love my clients. I love the work. But there are twenty-four hours in a day, seven days a week, and I was working more than one hundred hours a week.

"What has transpired after my year in the program is a lot of priming. I put together and wrote a complete operations manual, and as a result of doing that, we were able to train a brand-new assistant within days to fully support where we are today. We have transformed the way our bookkeeping is done and updated the website, which I'm really excited about. With all of that, our company income increased between 30 percent and 40 percent by year end.

"I believe in investing in myself and my business in the same way that I hope and expect people to invest in themselves by hiring me. I try to practice what I preach. And I very much believe in education and learning and doing better.

"If you care about your business and work-life balance, this is something that will provide that foundation and support for you."
—Suzanne Franchetti

Leverage Your Time

OBJECTIVE:

Be strategic about how you use your time by setting strong boundaries, reducing access and working only in your unique brilliance.

WHEN entrepreneurs first start their business, they're often flexible with clients, consenting to doing things outside of the original client agreement, doing extra work without charging for it, being available for phone calls on evenings or weekends, and granting unusual requests not within the original scope of work.

The problem is, once your client load is at full capacity and you have very little time, these extra (often non-paid) demands can take a toll on you, create resentment, and prevent you from growing your business further or enjoying your life.

Rather than putting out fires and focusing solely on the immediate, "urgent" tasks that provide only short-term, low-impact results, the solution is to reevaluate how you use your time in your business. Too often, entrepreneurs at this level give away their time, rather than using it strategically. You will now wish to set (and enforce) boundaries with the people in your life (personally and professionally) so you can use your time in the best way possible.

Doing this will help you gain back a surprising number of valuable hours which you can then use for visioning, strategizing, and implementing "important" long-term tasks, the ones that will make a significant impact on the long-term growth of your business, and help you enjoy your life again, with the ones you love.

> **1. At this phase of your business, time is your greatest currency and should be prized above all else.**

Not every minute of how you currently use your day has equal value. When you first start your business, it's an all-hands-on-deck approach: get done what you need to get done, grind it out, rinse, and repeat the following day. Everything needs to get done yesterday, and so you go to task, juggling fifteen balls in the air just to get past the start-up phase. You'll do anything that's required, because survival depends on you and only you.

Now that you've reached a new level in your business, this *modus operandi* no longer applies and, frankly, must stop. The way you used your time to get *here* isn't going to get you *there*, to that bigger next level. What's required is a shift in thinking about how you will use your time going forward.

Understanding that time is now your most precious commodity, you must embrace the fact that not every activity, task or project you work on provides an equal return on investment.

Here's what I mean: there are some things that you're currently working on in your business that are worth $100, $500, $1,000 or more per hour that truly only *you* can do in your business. In the Leveraged Business program, we call these Exponential Growth Activities (EGAs). I will explain these shortly.

Conversely, there are likely many other things you currently do during the day that you could easily pay someone else $15 an hour to do, maybe even $30 an hour. These we call Non-Exponential Growth Activities (NEGAs).

Understanding the difference in these types of activities is what can free you at this point:

- NEGAs are usually an *immediate gratification activity*, something that needs to get done but doesn't really add to the long-term growth of the business. These often involve putting out fires.
- Conversely, EGAs are typically more long-term, big vision-based, or rather involved business development activities and *slower gratification projects* that will take more time and will require your expertise or mastery to accomplish, rather than something you can quickly delegate.

When you make a list of all the tasks you currently work on in an average week and add next to each item the dollar amount you could pay someone else to complete these tasks, you notice that EGAs are worth far more in the long term of your business than NEGAs, for obvious reasons.

You also see where your time is actually going.

Here's the point I'm trying to make.

People complain about not having enough time to get everything done. This is not necessarily the problem. It's not that you don't have *enough time* to get everything done; you're simply now *working on the wrong things*. Categorizing the tasks on your to-do list to distinguish NEGAs from EGAs will help you use your time more effectively.

This new realization can help you make decisions about what you will and will no longer do, and allow you to be ruthless about how you use your time going forward. When you start focusing on more EGAs, you position your company for immense growth, both in terms of impact and financially.

Creating non-negotiable "EGA Days" is how you leverage your time and business. I have long believed that it's very difficult to build your business exponentially in between client appointments. Dealing with the "now" is a different type of thinking than that of being strategic and planning the future.

To grow, you must now shift your thinking and habits so as to create more uninterrupted blocks of time for EGAs, Exponential Growth Activities, as these are the ones that will free you from the cage you're in.

We call these EGA Days, and I have been using them in my business since the first few years of being self-employed. I realized that the more blocks of time I created for business development, rather than putting out fires or working on the immediate administrative tasks, the more serious traction I gained in my business.

In fact, the first year that I carved out a specific EGA Day in my calendar each week, I experienced a 35 percent increase in revenues within twelve months. This was a big revelation for me! When I leveraged my time, I increased my efforts and revenues.

Not long thereafter, I experienced a 300 percent increase in revenues in just twelve months using this same method, and a 530 percent increase in three years. It's not just for me, of course. The business owners we mentor now also experience a significant increase in revenues when they commit to doing this weekly. It is a revolutionary way to leverage your time for dramatic growth.

Why create blocks of time for long-term strategic work? It will help you be "in the flow" in terms of taking action on marketing ideas or projects that aren't necessarily urgent but that would significantly drive your business forward. Having these non-negotiable blocks of uninterrupted time helps you be intentional about the long-game of your business, rather than trying to squeeze it in whenever you have a couple of minutes.

Client example: A dental office we worked with to attract more patients was struggling to get any marketing done. The primary dentist was consistently busy working with patients and couldn't focus on client attraction—until we asked the office manager to schedule NO patients on Thursdays. At first, he resisted. *"How will I make more money if I'm working with patients one less day per week? That doesn't make sense to me."*

But very quickly, he realized that in the new block of time (a full day per week) he now had, he could focus on business development, marketing and setting up referral systems. He was actually able to put in place initiatives to drive more patients to his dental office, like finally being able to create his extensive website, send out letters to the human resource departments of large corporations in the vicinity, track and reward frequent referral sources, and host a bring-a-guest patient appreciation event that generated introductions and referrals to his dental practice, among other things.

Not too long thereafter, this extra time for focused strategy work each week provided him with the opportunity to see the potential for money he had been overlooking when he was too busy working with patients. He realized that cosmetic dentistry made his practice a lot more money than the typical cleanings and cavity work he had been focusing on before.

Based on this realization, he shifted his focus to bringing on more cosmetic dentistry patients and saw his revenues increase significantly. This allowed him to bring on more staff and increase the capacity of the dental practice, which again, increased his revenues.

Just ONE day per week to not work with patients improved everything for this dental practice. That's a great return on investment.

The Pareto Principle is alive and well in how you use your time. Are you familiar with the Pareto Principle, also known as the 80/20 rule? Essentially, it states that, for many events, roughly 80 percent of the effects come from only 20 percent of the causes. This is also known as the law of the vital few, and can be applied to your business.

As I became familiar with the Pareto Principle, I first began seeing it at play in my personal life. For example, I use only about 20 percent of my shoes 80 percent of the time; and when I travel, I often bring the same things, every time, all a small percentage of my entire wardrobe. And the list goes on and on.

But I also noticed it in my business: Only about 20 percent of my tasks were ones I enjoyed the most and 80 percent I would prefer not to do; 20 percent of my marketing activities seemed to bring me about 80 percent of my clients; approximately 20 percent of my clients gave me referrals consistently, etc.

The real breakthrough was when I realized that the way I used my time in my business dictated how much my business grew. It dawned on me that about *20 percent of my activities were what really drove the business forward significantly* (we call them Unique Brilliance activities), while 80 percent didn't have the same impact or value.

Wow.

It then occurred to me that if as much as 80 percent of results in my business ("outcomes") came from only 20 percent of my personal "activities," that there was a huge opportunity to shift how I used my time to simply do more of the activities on the 20 percent list.

Simply said, I could leverage my time by putting a pause button on the 80 percent of activities that produced poor results, while increasing the time I spent on the 20 percent of the activities that produced exceptional results.

That's when I began asking myself some strategic questions:

- Why was I wasting my valuable time on things that don't produce nearly the same results?

- What would happen if I transitioned to using exponentially more of my time on those things that did?

Eliminating the 80 percent of NEGA activities that brought me mediocre results and replacing them with EGA activities that previously only took up about 20 percent of my time created a *true compound effect.*

Not only was it revolutionary for my business based on how I used my own time, but we started applying it to the other members of my Team. If a certain team member produced 80 percent of their results for growing the business in only 20 percent of the use of their time, why couldn't we just get them to shift how they use their time to only work on their own EGAs?

It worked.

The lesson for your own business is this: instead of being reactive with how you use your time, notice how perhaps as much as 80 percent of your results may be coming from only 20 percent of your activities. What would happen to your business if you eliminated all the NEGAs (or at least delegated a large portion of them) and made a commitment to spend as much as 80 percent of your time on EGAs?

Would you too create a compound effect in how you leveraged your time? This is a way to completely shift the outcome of how you use your precious hours each day. It is also how you can go from overwhelmed at Six Figures to Seven Figures with your life back.

---

2. Do less, *better.*

"The difference between successful people and really successful people is that really successful people say no to almost everything."
—Warren Buffett

At this stage of business, the immediate money on the table is not as important as what's on the horizon. As we touched on previously, in the first stage of your business, you were in the "getting clients and making money" survival mode. You needed to focus on "money now" and couldn't afford to focus on future strategy.

You have now arrived at a different stage in your business, one in which the sole focus on "money now" is actually preventing you from growing exponentially.

With newer entrepreneurs not yet at the six-figure mark, we advise prioritizing their to-do list on activities that will provide them 1) the most money, 2) in the least amount of time to implement, 3) with the least effort on their part, and, 4) optionally, with the greatest long-term impact for the company.

(We call these Money Generating Activities, or MGAs.)

This might mean that it's most important to go networking, to have coffee with referral partners, to get booked to speak several times per month, and to create and market new programs for a quick infusion of cash. Whatever will bring in money, and fast!

The energy of MGAs are more urgent and reactive.

By all means, every business should focus on this in the early years and within our initial program, our coaches mentor early-stage business owners to focus on marketing, marketing, and *more* marketing and setting up systems so they attract clients consistently (i.e., Grow your online presence, Grow your stay-in-touch marketing, Grow your visibility, Grow your referrals, Grow your email list, Grow your platform, Grow your one-to-many offerings, Grow your speaking).

Money Generating Activities are crucial in the early stages.

But there's a point in your business (*now*, if you're in the Leverage phase) that this actually cripples you from working on the longer view. This is what happened to me. I was so busy working with individual clients, speaking, networking, creating and then launching countless small programs that I found myself with no bandwidth or capacity to focus on the strategic long-term growth projects.

Being at full-practice-capacity, I was stuck in "doing mode" and couldn't embrace "strategic mode." Things like shifting my branding to position my company for massive growth, writing a lead-generating business book, bringing on the right team members, or launching the personal-growth arm of my company went by the wayside.

The Exponential Growth Activities were consistently being put on the back burner.

That is, until I made a commitment to take a temporary step back from so much of the "doing" with the intent to focus on the things that were slower in the making, but would eventually help the business leap forward much further. This required saying no to a lot of things that were currently bringing in lots of money, which is admittedly a difficult decision to make. But I knew that, in my case, drawing a line in the sand and making a commitment to the future would pay off.

So, I stopped selling my best marketing product of all time; I stopped launching varied products on a monthly basis; I chose to do only *one* three-day conference per year, rather than the *three* I had previously done.

Yes, this choice was temporary and I knew full well it would slow down my revenues a bit, at least in the short term. But it was a strategic move to gain back more EGA time. Instead of using my days to market and launch countless little programs, I focused on a long-term, singular-growth path for the business, what is now the Leveraged Business program. I decided to *do less, better.*

And it paid off.

Simply said, saying no to bright shiny objects (*even* those that make money) allowed me to gain back my time to focus on doing *less*, but much *better.* And in turn, streamlining my business in this way allowed it to grow and set itself up to run a lot more without my direct involvement. (By the way, this is a method for making more, working less.)

How do you prioritize what activities to work on now that you're at the Leverage stage of your business? It's not the same "early stage business" Money Generating Activities formula as I shared with you earlier.

It's flipped on its head to focus on Exponential Growth Activities, where you aim to focus on projects that will provide 1) the greatest long-term impact for the company, and then on, 2) what will bring in the most money, 3) in the least amount of time to implement, 4) with the least effort on your part.

Notice that it is taking the previously "optional" focus of working on long-term impact projects, and making it a priority at this stage of your business. Doing this allows you to focus on what matters more: you being in a *strategic role* versus a *delivery role*, as we will discuss soon.

Caveat: This does not mean that you *stop* working with clients or focusing on the bread-and-butter of your business. You must still focus on doing the activities that bring in money, and you'll certainly continue to market and to sign on new clients. It simply means saying no to the *extraneous* or bright shiny objects (for the short term) so you can focus more of your time on EGAs and achieve exponential growth.

Be strategic here and think it through, so you don't find yourself without any cash coming in.

That being said, even though the immense satisfaction of "immediate cash" isn't as present, be reassured that the long-term planning will likely cover the backward step you took to help you jump further in the near future. It will be worth it. You must do *less*, but *better*. This is leverage.

You don't get results from things you don't finish. Over the years of working with thousands of business owners at different stages of business, and after seeing an overwhelming trend in their assessment results, I've come to learn that the majority of us entrepreneurs love to *start* new things but aren't necessarily wired to *finish* what we start. We are often high-idea generators, but not always consistent about dotting every "i" and crossing every "t."

Once something has been started, a project often loses its magic for typical entrepreneurs, which causes a loss of momentum as they move their attention and focus on another project, idea, or even start another business.

This is *normal*, in the sense that it is common practice, but it does slow down business growth, causing it to plateau at a certain level. So, if you're wondering why growth isn't happening fast enough, not finishing what you've already started is likely one of the reasons.

I've long believed and shouted from the rooftops that you don't get results from things you don't implement fully. Yes, there is a great feeling of forward-movement as you're starting a project and making headway on it. But if that project is never completed, you might as well not have started it at all.

For example: If you begin writing a book that will give your business exposure and visibility, but only get it halfway written, you won't get the new speaking gigs or clients you would have gotten if you had actually *published* it or made it available online as a lead-generation tool. In fact, nothing will likely change, even if you've spent six months or even three years writing it.

If you create your signature talk but never get a chance to deliver it in front of an audience, it won't produce results. If you meet ideal new referral partners at a networking group but never reach out to them to collaborate on the project you discussed, you might as well have stayed home that day. Sad, but true.

Every time we add yet another project (or a new business) to our already-full plate, *we delay the completion of everything else that is presently on our plate*, which doesn't bring us closer to where we want to be.

For a change to happen, and for you to produce more with less effort, the mindset shift required is your willingness to *complete what you start*. If this requires starting fewer things (three instead of ten) then that's what needs to happen, even if it goes against how you typically do things.

It is better to focus on a *few* things and crush the results by fully implementing them than to focus on too many things and not finish them fully, which produces no results.

That being said, this doesn't mean that you have to take every project to 100 percent completion on your own. Many business owners, including myself, just aren't wired to do that, at least not solo.

Instead, you can set up your environment to take a certain project to 70 or 80 percent completion and *then* ask for help. If it means getting support in staying on task, then by all means get that support. But focus on the completion of fewer big projects and you will find that it takes less of your time, for greater results, which is the ultimate leverage of your time.

---

3. To scale your business further, stop people-pleasing.

You don't owe anyone *anything*. If you are among those who are overwhelmed and feeling crushed under their to-do lists, commitments or client workload, it may not just be a question of too much volume or a need to prioritize better.

It may also be a symptom that you've put the needs of others before your own.

Some kind-hearted business owners want to be liked so much that they agree to do things, or give their time to others beyond what they actually *want* to give, so they can feel appreciated and significant, or because *"It's the right thing to do"* or even because *"They asked so nicely, and I didn't feel I could say no."*

Truth be told, and this is almost never talked about in traditional business circles, this form of *overgiving to the point of sacrifice or martyrdom* often comes from the subconscious need to fill the gap around *not feeling good enough*, a belief in *not being enough*, or that *one's worth is proven* by sacrificing one's time or personal boundaries.

In the Leveraged Business program, when we teach the Leverage Your Time Activator over a two-day period, we put a strong focus on helping business owners to say no. We embrace the philosophy that *setting boundaries is an act of self-love.*

Doing this is transformative, not just in terms of time, but also of increasing self-worth.

If you understand that your value is a birthright, that your innate worth can never be taken from you, and you begin to love, honor and value yourself and your needs (as I teach in the first chapter of my book, *Embrace Your Magnificence*), then you will realize that you don't *need* to people-please to be liked.

When you like yourself, you don't need to give of yourself endlessly to be liked by others. When you love yourself, that's *enough*. This applies to your business as well.

I'd like to give you permission to be bolder about meeting your own needs *first* and to simply say no to things you simply don't *want* to do, don't have *time* for, or that aren't in alignment with your greatest professional goals or personal aspirations.

That means that you may want to announce to that board of directors that you'll be stepping down next month; that you will stop going to that networking group that's an hour and a half away and hasn't produced results in a year. It will also mean that you find a way to get out of hosting an event you got talked into but don't want to do.

And, dare I say it as you might judge my parenting for saying this, it may mean that you tell your family that you can no longer be the one driving the kids to countless soccer practices, baseball games and swim meets *during work hours* (and even on evenings and weekends) as I did.

You are a business owner, not a chauffeur. Self-employed does *not* mean unemployed. You have important work to do. (I realize this can be a lot to take in with the societal pressure that, especially we women, are put under. Just breathe.)

Yes, you can *choose* to give your time to charities, to benevolent projects, to your community and family, but let that be *your choice*, not because someone blindly expects you to do it, or asks nicely, especially when you feel you should be working on growing your business.

The same goes for clients. You don't *owe* clients anything other than what is expressly agreed between you or what's in writing. This is taking up way more of your time than you think, and is eating into your Exponential Growth Activity focus time (more on that later).

The bottom line is, if you find yourself complaining that you don't have enough time to grow your business, you may want to reevaluate how you actually use your time.

If you were to make a list of all the unnecessary or unpaid time you give your clients, community, people who just *"want to pick your brain,"* and volunteering endlessly, and you were to add up all those hours you give away each week and then multiply that number by fifty-two weeks, you would find that you would have *plenty* of time to focus on the growth of your business.

It's about being bolder and creating stronger boundaries, something that comes with a bit of practice, but works very, very well.

Be unapologetic about taking back your time from those you've allowed to hijack it. This is your permission to take your life back, unapologetically. If you've been playing the role of "people pleaser" or "good girl/good boy," this may admittedly ruffle your feathers at first. You may fear that people will think you're rude or selfish by saying no, and that ultimately, they won't like you for it.

But here's the deal: if certain people only like you because of things you do for them for free, that's not friendship; it's abuse. If people only spend time with you because you overgive without reward, that's also abuse and I believe it needs to stop, for your benefit.

You're worth so much more than that and you deserve to be appreciated for your qualities and your personality instead of the fact that you can be taken advantage of, by clients, vendors, team members, or people in general, including family.

That being said, it's time to clear the decks and start saying no more often, which can be really tricky for some people, *especially women*, even already successful business owners.

First, know that you don't need an excuse to remove yourself from an obligation that no longer serves you or from something that someone requested of you.

You can just say:

- *"Thank you for thinking of me. I will not be able to do that. Best of luck going forward."*
- *"I'm so honored you thought of me first. I will decline your invitation but I know you'll find someone just perfect for the role."*
- *"I will no longer be able to (insert thing you committed to). Thank you for allowing me to be a part of it all this time."*

The key in communicating this is to do it without needing to say *anything else* or explain yourself further. If you try to explain why you're setting the boundary or use an excuse, it will invite the person you're setting a boundary with to negotiate with you.

Be grateful for the opportunity, but firm about your answer. If they press and ask why, you still don't need to give a reason, just *"It's something I'm choosing not to do at this time."*

Then, be comfortable with the awkward (sometimes excruciating) silence that will follow for about two seconds. This may be one of the most difficult things you will have to do in your business, or your life, but it will strengthen muscles in your mindset that will help you leverage your business and gain your life back, now and for many years to come.

It will also dramatically increase your sense of self-worth and personal fulfillment, which will affect your business for the rest of your career.

---

4. Setting strong boundaries helps you grow your business exponentially.

Others aren't responsible for how they treat you (or your time), *you are.* I know this may initially be difficult to hear, but in the personal-growth and development work that I do with individuals who don't have a business, I stress that the way someone treats you is simply the result of how you have taught them or allowed them to treat you. The same is true in your business.

If someone has hijacked your time and continues to do so, it's because they're not clear about your standards (your personal rules) around what's acceptable and what's not. Meaning, you simply have not educated them around how to deal with you in your interactions.

If a handful of your clients or customers feel entitled to call you on your mobile phone into the evening and on weekends, and this frustrates you and eats up your time, both personal and professional, this is not something that will end on its own.

That client will continue to use that privilege *until you do something about it.*

In the first few years of my business, I offered my one-on-one clients unlimited email access in between our phone calls. Here's what I discovered: approximately 20 percent of my clients never used this unlimited access, 60 percent used it occasionally and within reason, and the other 20 percent were the ones who used it consistently, sometimes even abused it.

These were the clients who wrote me lengthy emails or who sent me their 150-page book manuscript, with a note that said, *"Please read and let me know what you think,"* even though this would take countless hours of my time, was outside of our scope of work or agreement, and I wouldn't be compensated.

It just didn't seem fair and I felt taken advantage of, growing more and more resentful each time I agreed to these requests that served them but not me. Over time, I realized it was my fault this was continuing to happen because I was the one who had agreed to their request the first few times they asked. I knew that I needed to revisit our working relationship and *educate them* that we were going to be changing the way we would be working together going forward. It was the only way to gain back control of my time.

Here's what I did, so that perhaps you can do the same too.

First, I drafted up my new list of standards for "what's acceptable and what's not acceptable" in our dealings with each other, i.e. boundaries. I then turned them into my set of policies and procedures, essentially communicating "how we do things around here," wording it as nicely as I could. Next, I drafted them up into a document that I shared with existing clients, which was included in the welcome packet all new clients received and were required to sign off on to be able to move forward in working with me.

This series of steps was life-changing for me. My clients got the message and the majority of them were absolutely respectful of my new policies. The one client who wasn't okay with this new way of working with me left grumbling and complaining, and I was thrilled to see him go. Needless to say, he knew all along that he'd been taking advantage of me. We both did.

Truth be told, it's *always* easier to educate new clients or team members about new boundaries, rather than trying to do so with people who've gotten used to dealing with you in a certain way. The good news is that it can be done.

Sometimes, a longtime client who's been abusing your time won't like your new standards and will walk away from your working relationship. That can be a great blessing as it clears your calendar for new, better clients who will honor your new way of working, or to focus on important activities that will leverage your business even further.

Enforcing your boundaries is *self-esteem in action*. Having boundaries is all well and good, but if they're not enforced, they might as well not exist. I believe that one of the reasons most people don't have boundaries in the first place is that they're afraid they'll have to enforce them, and that means playing "the bad cop," the one person no one really likes.

Enforcing your stated boundaries is not about being unlikable, cold or heartless. It's about standing firm on what you believe, and taking a stand for what's important to you. It's *self-esteem in action*. If you think about people who have strong boundaries and enforce them with kindness, the likelihood is that you actually have respect for them, that you admire how they care for themselves, and that it's actually more comfortable to be around them, because you always know where you stand.

For an oil lamp to keep burning brightly, the oil container needs to be refilled continually. The same goes with you. As it relates to your business, you can't keep providing value to your clients and customers if you're physically and emotionally depleted because someone is taking advantage of you.

When boundary issues or warning signs appear, address these issues with the client quickly. Be sensitive to their feelings when doing this, but also stay firm. If they trespass a boundary, send them an email reminding them about a stated policy (boundary). Perhaps, if this is the first time they've trespassed it, you may "let it slip this time" by giving them a get-out-of-jail-free card, as I used to say with a smile. At the same time, I would let them know that the next time it happened I would follow through on the stated policy. Clients usually found that this was fair and appreciated the reminder.

By all means, make yourself available for clients if there is an emergency. Sink into your heart, have compassion, and be of service, but beware of clients who will repeatedly take advantage of you and your kindness. The key is to be *kind,* but also *firm.* I often tell my clients (and my children certainly know this about me too) that "I'm loving, but *not* lenient."

Ideally, *you* are not the one playing the bad cop. Your assistant or office manager should do the bad cop job so you can continue being the good cop. This means that your assistant is the one delivering the news that something isn't working and gently reminding your client about what's acceptable and not acceptable, as stated in the policies and procedures.

And not every client will follow your new boundaries. That being said, it's perfectly acceptable to fire a client who doesn't behave. The client is *not* always right. Some "saboteur clients" will never adhere to your policies and will wreak havoc on your schedule and your team's time. Step in and say something. If that doesn't change the behavior, then it's time to lovingly release them back into the world so they can find someone else better suited for them.

It goes without saying, *you will always be your worst enemy around boundaries*, especially if you are a compassionate person, someone who seeks harmony or avoids confrontation. That said, if you don't enforce your own standards and boundaries, saboteur clients won't take you seriously and they will keep creating problems in your business, while eating up your most valuable resource: the time you need to build your business even further, and the time to enjoy the things (and people) you love.

Leverage your time in this way and you can scale your business and gain your life back.

---

5. Reducing access is beneficial for you and your clients.

Beware of taking on the "rescuer" role. A big mindset shift that must occur if you're committed to leveraging your business and gaining your freedom back is to realize that you are responsible *to* your clients but not *for* them, or their results. This can be a big pill to swallow at first, because many business owners feel that their role is to *save the client.*

This is not true. You are not here to rescue your clients. Your role is to give clients what you agreed to give them, and under no circumstances does this include giving them your proverbial first-born child.

Playing the role of the rescuer or superhero leads to exhaustion, burnout or "compassion fatigue" that comes from lack of sleep or anxiety related to the client's situation. It also leads to enabling your client to not take ownership for their part of the working relationship and sets up a codependent one instead, which ultimately does not serve them.

Yes, playing the "rescuer" role feels good for a while because it makes you feel like a hero. It is tied into the ego feeling significant and that you are here to save the day, continually. But unless you have a done-for-you business, what you're doing in the process is akin to energetically crippling the client, not allowing them to take personal responsibility for their results or their life. It's the equivalent of severely over-protecting a child. Doing this doesn't prepare them for the realities of life in adulthood.

One of the first things I teach in the program is the concept of *personal responsibility*, that everyone is responsible for their own outcomes, and that you create your life with every *action*, as well as every *inaction*.

Imagine hiring a nutritionist who invites you to eat more green vegetables, drink more water, replace packaged and processed foods with organic whole foods and move your body more often. Imaging now that, instead of following their sound advice, you sit on your sofa morning to night, eating buckets of greasy processed food and guzzling soda by the liter. In the end, it is *your* responsibility, not theirs, if you don't get the results you initially signed up for, correct?

The same goes with your clients and customers.

Assuming that you set up your products, programs, or offerings with integrity, knowing that you've included everything you can to practically "guarantee" results if applied fully, your clients' outcomes are *their* personal responsibility, not yours. This means that you are responsible for giving them what you promised, and yet, in the end, the outcome is based on their choices.

This is usually difficult to own if you're a business owner who's played the rescuer role for many years and you feel important as a result of doing so. Problem is, this is tiring and not sustainable for the long run. If you want to overcome "compassion fatigue" and gain your time back, a mindset shift around overgiving must be made, along with the appropriate actions of letting the client be more responsible for their own results.

You are likely giving too much access to your clients. Whenever we are working with a new member in the program who is overwhelmed and drowning in their business, we examine their business model and how they actually deliver the work to their clients. Often, the clue is right there: their clients have an unnecessary *overabundance of access* to the business owner.

Many entrepreneurs in the early stages of their business believe that clients can only get great results if they are holding their hand the whole time. This happened to me too. We worry that without our consistent personal presence, the client will not get what they're paying for.

This is not true. In fact, if we're being honest, being available to your clients 24/7 is often driven by fear on the business owner's part: fear of not being able to control an outcome, of not feeling needed, and, for some, a deeply hidden fear of loss of love or abandonment, often replaying itself from childhood.

What we almost always discover with our members experiencing this is that their clients don't actually *need* as much time with them as the business owner originally thought. Yes, the client *wants* it because it's been made available to them, but they don't actually require it. An associate or "junior you" can take over after some time, perhaps after the initial meeting. When the proverbial baton has been passed, you are free to spend your time moving your business forward again, rather than babysitting a client.

Here's what this can look like: a website designer or interior designer can initially be the one to meet with the new client, understand their problem, design the website layout or room decor strategy, and then the junior designer can step in to finish the work, under the designer's supervision of course.

When the client understands this procedure upfront, and that the junior designer is the person to contact on a daily basis after the initial round of meetings, they feel comfortable with the process. The upside (and you can communicate this to them) is that instead of only working with one person, this arrangement gives them a team of professionals working on their account.

When we do remove access little by little, either by slowly taking it away, replacing your support with that of another team member, or automating it with technology, we notice that the clients *still get results*.

Certainly, an education process is needed if a client has been used to working with you a certain way; an education process that involves you teaching your clients how to get results without you being available at all times of day or night. Instead of handing them a fish, you support them to fish by themselves or get the fish from your assistant, rather than from you. This will serve them much better going forward, especially if you are already difficult to reach.

What you must realize in removing access is that you will be more resistant to it than the client will be. It's more about you being okay with letting go and not being as available for daily handholding.

If you aren't yet comfortable removing 24/7 type support from your clients, save this "unlimited access" option for those who pay a hefty premium for it, with some sort of VIP program. Even then, access must be kept to a reasonable amount if you want to leverage your business further.

A business that requires you (especially 24/7) is *not* a leveraged business. Embracing this concept and actually reducing your availability, or providing a replacement for you, is another important aspect of leveraging your time so that you can focus it on building your business.

What's the impact of applying the Time Activator in your business? Alan explains it to you in his own words:

"We own a brand design company where we help clients dissect who they are and rebuild their brand from their core values and purpose, so they can be remarkable and attract the appropriate clients.

"I was struggling, both internally and externally, with finding a purpose and knowing what I wanted to do with my business and my life. I had extreme ups and downs with my business and I could never seem to get beyond a certain level. It was extremely frustrating.

"I sensed that there was something more out there that I just wasn't understanding. One day, I said, 'I just want enlightenment. Give me something.' The next day, I got the weekly email newsletter from Fabienne about a three-day event she was hosting. I attended that event and in the middle of the first day, I called my wife and said, 'Oh my gosh, I think this is everything I've been looking for.' Pieces started falling into place.

"I thought I was a failure, and I thought of money as a bad thing from my childhood. I realized that I wasn't alone in that thinking, and that if you flip that thinking, you can start creating your life and your business. You get a completely different approach to life.

"I had hit quite a low in my life. I didn't know what to do anymore. I was so desperate. I hated my journey and I hated my life. To be quite honest, if I hadn't found this program, things would be much, much different.

"Today, I love my journey. I get up at 4:30 every morning because I'm excited about what will happen that day. I don't resist things. If I expect a certain thing to happen that day and it doesn't happen, I don't get upset. I go with the flow, and I've got a bigger vision than I've ever had for my business. If something doesn't quite work out, I don't freak out like I used to.

"I've got things in perspective. I know what I'm doing. I'm very focused. My time is used very wisely. I can prioritize things. I used to be overwhelmed all the time but I'm not anymore. I'm very intentional with what I do. I used to work sixty-plus hours per week, but now, I get up early because I want to.

"I go meet my daughter at the bus at 4:00 p.m., and that's the end of my day. I work Monday through Friday, and, actually, now I'm taking Fridays as my self-care and clarity break day. I'm still getting everything done. I'm not overwhelmed and my business is thriving, though we've still got a lot of things we want to accomplish.

"I feel like I'm back in high school when I was excited about life and the potential of things.

"Your thoughts can become things. You have to have a vision. Then you have to believe in your vision, and then take action. I used to have ideas and I might have taken sporadic actions, but I didn't believe in myself. I'd get really excited, and then when I wouldn't get what I thought I would get, I would crash and get upset.

"Now, it's the thought, the belief, and the action, trusting in my journey and just being able to dissect differently than what I did before. I create a framework around the vision now. I let the 'how it's going to get done' work itself out. I focus on the moment each day.

"I now have the framework and the big vision, and I just let things happen. As long as I'm always moving forward with intention, I can see the opportunities along the way. Before, I wouldn't really see them. I'd think I would see them, or I'd know how it would need to be, but that wasn't the right way.

"I'm now leveraging my unique brilliance and having other people do the things that I really am not the best at. I've learned to give things up and let people help. I used to do everything myself, but by only doing what I do best, and allowing others to do things to help me do what I do best, my business infrastructure has come to life, along with my mind.

"I have a better relationship with my family and I feel better about myself as a result of it. I dream bigger for my business, and I'm hitting bigger goals as a result of it as well. It's been life changing for me." —Alan Wallner

Leverage Your
Business Model

OBJECTIVE:

Shift how you deliver your work so you are no longer working hours-for-dollars and can work with two to ten times your current number of clients, while working fewer hours.

AT THIS POINT in your business, it is likely impossible for you to grow exponentially. Could you handle ten times the number of clients tomorrow (as it relates to your current business model/delivery method)?

A few years ago, when the movie *The Secret* came out and experienced extensive viewership, rumor had it that many of the business owners featured in this popular documentary experienced so much visibility as a result of their appearance in the film that their businesses couldn't handle the exposure. Some of these businesses were not set up to handle all of the unexpected interest. Their business models (and systems or structures) were not ready to accept that many new clients, and a significant opportunity was lost.

How you *deliver* your work to clients and customers matters more than you might think. Your current business model most likely cannot be scaled, and yet by shifting your business model, you can be ready to experience exponential growth, at the same time as exponential down time.

> ## 1. Multiplying your number of clients or customers is the right thing to do.

By keeping your existing business model the same, you are depriving countless people of your beneficial solutions. At this moment, somewhere on the planet, there are legions of people or organizations that could use what you have to offer. They have a problem that you can solve, but you're too "small" to be able to help all of them. You are likely keeping yourself back because you're at full capacity, not able to take on that much more work without imploding.

Right now, you've chosen one business model, but it likely has you feeling trapped. What you may not know is that there are literally countless different possible permutations for how you could deliver your solutions or services in a beneficial way, without having all the results *or* delivery depend entirely on you.

For some business owners, scaling the business exponentially could be the equivalent of a moral obligation. Here's what I mean. I'd like you to imagine that you have stumbled upon the cure for cancer. You know your methodology works, and that you help each person you work with individually to heal. Deep down, you wish everyone could have access to this method, but right now, there's no more of you or your time to go around. Your current delivery process (meaning, your business model) dictates that you can only work one-to-one with up to twenty clients at one time.

Your argument could be, *"Yes, I have the cure for a disease that could revolutionize the world if I could work with lots more people, but I can't do that because I must deliver it one-to-one for it to work. There is no other way."*

Valid? Perhaps with your current business model, yes. But we've worked with many health practitioners and healers within our programs who originally believed only they could deliver their work the way they currently do, otherwise *"It wouldn't work."* Meanwhile, they were leaving a lot of money on the table, burning the candle at both ends and most importantly, not making themselves available to so many more people who need them.

So, they would stay stuck at twenty clients, when they could be able to have an impact on two hundred or two thousand people's lives at a time, if only they shifted their business model.

A belief like *"It wouldn't work"* is something I call a Sacred Cow, a belief that you hold as untouchable and unchangeable, even though it's just a belief and *beliefs can be changed.* These deeply held beliefs of there being only one way to deliver a service (and it's usually *"the way it's always been done, and for good reason"*) are simply *not* true, no matter the industry.

When there's a will, there is always a way, especially when we are willing to be creative. First, it requires a shift in mindset, a willingness to see things differently and to try a different approach. Once that shift is made, usually by challenging existing beliefs, the new leveraged business model shows up, one that helps us work one-to-many versus one-to-one and we can begin doing this work in a much greater, exponential capacity.

Here's my gentle argument back to the *"It won't work any other way"* rationale: assuming that what you do genuinely helps people, is good for them, provides true value, makes their lives better than before, provides a future result they want or brings a benefit to the planet, the more individuals or companies you serve, the more you make the world a better place. *There is a moral obligation to make this available to more people.* Therefore, holding yourself back from growth is not doing anyone any good.

Let's stay with the cancer example for a moment.

Imagine all the tens of thousands, even millions of people with cancer and their family members whose lives would be positively affected by your methodology. Imagine them waking up every night with a cold sweat, in fear and praying for a solution to their health challenge. The only two reasons they're not solving their problem (curing their cancer) are 1) they don't know about you and your method yet (an issue of marketing), and 2) you haven't switched to a business model that is leveraged enough to provide your solution to many more people than the original fifteen to twenty that you have capacity for now (an issue of delivery, or business model).

The solution to both of these has to do with you deciding to do things differently going forward, even if it means stepping outside of your comfort zone.

If you're a logical person, it might make sense that helping more clients and customers is a moral obligation. If you're a spiritual person, it may feel like a divine obligation. And if you're financially driven, it may simply feel like a financial obligation, to your employees, their families, and your own family.

Either way, my message to you around your business model is that *you cannot be of service to more people and leverage your revenues and impact on the world if you stay working one-to-one.* The goal therefore is to clone and multiply YOU or what you provide, *infinitely*, so you can help as many people as possible to have a better life.

Getting out of your current comfort zone will help you work with ten to one hundred times more people. Most entrepreneurs start their business as the *Doer*, the jack-of-all-trades. They set up their business from the *"I will do the work because I'm good at it and I like doing it"* mindset. Sadly, this is where most stop, some spending their entire career in one particular delivery model, with no exit strategy at the end of their career, because everything depended on them doing the work.

A few eventually hire other people to do the work, which allows them to take the role of *Manager*, rather than the Doer, to create systems, processes and then build a talented team that eventually frees up the entrepreneur to no longer deliver all the work, allowing them to focus on expansion and make more, working far less.

Sadly, very few ever experience this because old rules dictate the future. They stop themselves by thinking, *"Well, this is the way we've always done it,"* or *"This is how we do things in my industry. It wouldn't work any other way."*

But what if we were to wipe clean your existing thinking about how you do business and think beyond your existing comfort zone? The Tabula Rasa exercise, as we call it in the program, is your opportunity to release the shackles of past decisions that may be preventing you from scaling your business, even if only on paper for now.

To achieve this and expand your thinking, here are several questions you can ask yourself now:

1) *What would need to shift in my business for my company to provide our product or service to ten times the number of clients or customers we work with now?*

2) *What other industries or segments of the population need what we provide, beyond who we serve now?*

3) *What would need to change to be able to provide my solution beyond my existing geographic limitations, across the globe?*

4) *Who is already doing this, in my industry or in another industry? How?*

5) *How could I remove ME in the delivery and replace myself with others or rely more heavily on technology?*

There are lots more people (or companies, industries, etc.) who need what you have to offer way beyond the current geographic area or type of client you're currently limited to. To greatly multiply your business and add another zero to your yearly revenues, put a focus on replacing you and then eventually multiplying your process by ten or one hundred times in all capacities, including marketing, sales, delivery, referral generation, exposure, product creation, manufacturing, etc.

Doing so may seem overwhelming at first, especially if you have no direction or haven't done this before, and you attempt to tackle it alone. But with the right strategy, support and accountability, you can put one foot in front of the other and within a relatively short period of time, you can shift things to be able to serve so many more people.

It simply requires a shift in mindset and a willingness to get out of your current comfort zone. *Everything you seek is on the other side of this.*

---

2. You are not the only one who can deliver your work to the world.

It's time to embrace the "Mini-Me Mentality." Even though you (perhaps rightfully) believe you are the *only one* who can do what you do for your clients and customers, there are countless others who are capable of doing it too, some just as well as you, if given the chance. There are skilled people out there secretly begging to slide into an *already existing platform and process*, not wishing to reinvent the wheel you're currently using.

Meaning, there are people out there who would love to work for you and help deliver your work to your clients and customers. They are uniquely positioned to sell your products, consult with your clients, work with your patients, facilitate your groups, and would relish the opportunity to do it for you without having to run a business on their own.

Even though they're perfectly capable of having their own business doing what you do, many would prefer never to have to start a process from scratch, deal with the marketing and sales, or manage people or operations. They would prefer to work with existing systems, not be in charge of hiring or firing, handling employees or worrying about making payroll every week.

Not everyone is wired to take big risks, as you likely have been. Not everyone is happy being a dragon slayer. Some people would be delighted to be your "mini-me." For them, it would be an honor to be your trained clone or license an existing solution that works (such as yours). They prefer to avoid all those headaches. They're happy to just do the "client-facing work," the work you are currently doing all by yourself now.

Allowing someone else to come into your business to do the work you are currently doing requires a mindset shift, mainly, that you are *not* the only one who can provide the result. Once you embrace the mindset that someone else can do the delivery for you, in a very qualified way, you will find the person and, eventually, many people who will do it happily for you.

There are also many ways of delivering what you offer using associates, facilitators, automated technology systems and software solutions, licensing, franchising, or online delivery of products and courses. In fact, the possibilities for providing solutions to many, many more people are endless.

Again, what's required is believing that you are *not* the only one who can physically provide the result and embracing a business model that does it for you, whether it's through other people, software, or through any other means.

It's time for your company to expand from working one-to-one or with a very small number of people to working with hundreds if not tens of thousands of people. It starts with a decision and commitment to change your business model through a shift in how you see delivering your work in the world and with the right guidance and direction.

Michelangelo understood the difference between Art and Craft. Art history teaches us that Michelangelo hired a large number of assistants throughout his career. Working on the Sistine Chapel ceiling, several assistants prepared plaster, mixed paints, and climbed up and down ladders to deliver him supplies.

When Michelangelo felt that an assistant had enough talent to actually paint, he would allow the assistant to paint a part of the landscape, a patch of sky or a small figure. One of Michelangelo's longtime assistants, Pietro Urbino, worked with him for over twenty-five years and helped him with a number of important works we think of today as solely Michelangelo's works.

Michelangelo is known worldwide as a masterful artist, one of the greatest of all time, and yet he was aided by a skilled craftsman for most of his career. We believe and assume that he "delivered" 100 percent of the work he is known for, but in fact, he didn't. He only delivered a percentage of it: the *vision* and the *art*, as opposed to simply the craft.

There is an Art and a Craft in your business too.

With an Artist, we think of innovation, mastery, heart, passion, unique brilliance, intuition, innate talent, expression, magic, alchemy, something singular that can only be communicated or produced by one person in one way. *The vision.*

In thinking about a Craftsman, on the other hand, we think of a skilled manual worker, someone who learns how to produce something functional, who learns a trade using his hands. We think of a job or activity that requires a skill that can be repeated. *The hands that do the work.*

In the delivery of successful results, many business owners blindly believe that *they alone* must be responsible for 100 percent of the work. Because of this, they stay stuck in a one-to-one model, being able to work with only a few clients or customers, because there are only so many hours in the day and only so much of the business owner to go around.

This is not true, not in a leveraged business.

A few years ago, my husband Derek experienced an injury in both of his knees while skiing in Colorado. He had torn his ACL and meniscus in both knees and flew home to New York City to have surgery with one of the best-reputed orthopedic surgeons in the U.S., especially among professional athletes. The surgeon met with Derek for an incredibly short period of time, quickly established the injury in both knees, leaving the appointment after no more than five minutes. In came the second-in-command.

Post-operation, the surgeon once again came in to check on Derek for about ninety seconds, then shook his hand, smiled and said goodbye.

Both surgeries turned out very well and my husband felt he had "brand-new knees." But it dawned on us that the famed surgeon didn't do *all* of the work. His aides did a majority of it, under his strict supervision and using his proprietary, innovative methods, the ones for which this surgeon is known worldwide. Sounds a lot like Michelangelo.

We teach our business owners that Craft is a *process that produces results.* (We'll talk about The Reliable Results Process™ shortly.) Craft is *"how we do things around here to produce a desired result,"* the procedure, the proven methodology, the system we follow.

Craft doesn't require intuition or magic. It's a formula, based on the original innovation or vision, that can be replicated and followed by someone else with similar results. And Craft can be as much as 80 percent of the reason for an outcome, sometimes even 100 percent.

The other 20 percent is Art, the vision, the innovation, the added *je ne sais quoi* that only you can provide.

And here's the piece I would like for you to really get. You can *teach someone else* to do the 80 percent of the Craft or delivery, and then come in and do the last 20 percent of the Art. Or vice versa: begin the process with 20 percent of Art (like a diagnosis or drafting up the plans) and then allow someone to finish it with the remaining 80 percent of Craft.

Either way, clients don't always *need* 100 percent of what you (the business owner) currently provide them in order to get the results they seek. Eighty percent can be taught or done by someone else, duplicated or automated, depending on your type of business and industry. You can even decide whether that last 20 percent of Art is crucial for *you* to do, or if you do indeed want to do it. It's up to you.

Entrepreneurs often say, *"But they will never do it like me!"* and if you are thinking this too, you are correct. No one will do it exactly like you. You are uniquely brilliant at some aspects of what you do. But as one of my mentors once told me, *"Good is good enough."* Sometimes, 80 percent is better than zero percent.

But perhaps someone else who is talented can take over the 20 percent of Art you used to provide. Every person has their own set of gifts and unique brilliance, and while no other person can replicate yours exactly, they come with their own.

To follow our earlier analogy that relates to having the cure for cancer, I will ask you this: would you rather have a dozen people experience a cure because *you* were the one who was responsible for helping them, or tens of thousands, because you had special elves delivering the work with you?

---

3. Every business has in its DNA a Reliable Results Process™.

You are not personally responsible for your clients' results, *your process is*. Yes, you're good at what you do for your clients because, in part, it comes naturally to you. In fact, you've been doing this for so long that it's most likely an intuitive process. The problem is, this intuitive process lives largely in your head. It requires you, your time and your focused personal attention. Which means that it's not necessarily scalable.

But a proven process *is* scalable.

The way for you to get out of your current business model and leverage your business is to document every single step of the process by which you currently create reliable results for your clients. (This is a different documentation process than the systems and operations we talked about earlier regarding how your business runs.)

Again, you may be thinking, *"No, a documented process won't work in my business. Every client and customer of mine is different, they have different issues and they all need highly customized solutions. A one-size-fits-all model would never work for me!"* You wouldn't be the first to think this. In my experience, many business owners have the initial belief that, without their highly intuitive role in the process of creating highly customized solutions, clients can't get positive results.

Yes, it may be true that all clients *could* benefit from highly customized solutions, but it's not the *only* path to predictable results.

Here's what I mean:

In my first business, a holistic health and nutrition coaching business I called Natural Transformations, I helped people eat more whole foods and, when possible, helped them with their chronic health concerns by changing their diet and lifestyle choices.

One day, a woman came in with elevated cholesterol numbers and wanted to change her diet to aid her recovery, along with what she and her doctor were doing together. Up until that point in my business, I had mostly helped people lose weight and gain energy by consuming whole foods. That being said, I'd never specifically treated a cholesterol problem before and wasn't yet familiar with what particular foods to recommend, which I admitted to her. She was still interested in getting my help.

Undeterred, I pulled from my bookshelf an encyclopedia-sized natural healing book, with health concerns listed from A to Z. We flipped to the cholesterol section and I handed her the book and asked her to read the food recommendation paragraphs while I took notes for her, including how to source these foods and cook them in a way to make them taste good.

The book recommended reducing the consumption of meat, dairy, sugar, processed foods, soda, and caffeine, among other things. At the same time, it recommended consuming more whole grains, organic vegetables, leafy greens, beans, sea vegetables, and water.

After she confirmed this with her doctor who gave her a thumbs up, we both went to task, me teaching her how to cook brown rice without making it stick to the pot, how to steam kale and dress it so she would like it, and make better lifestyle choices overall. Every two weeks, she came in for our session and grew a repertoire of healthy food preparations and "cleaner" living.

Over a short period of time, she was happier, clearer, she slimmed down considerably and got positive news about the cholesterol from her doctor. We were thrilled.

Not too long afterward, a client came in with anemia, another health concern I hadn't experienced or treated before. I grabbed the book again and we flipped to the anemia section, and among other things, the book recommended reducing the consumption of meat, dairy, sugar, processed foods, soda, and caffeine, and recommended consuming more whole grains, organic vegetables, leafy greens, beans, sea vegetables, and water. She too got better.

Then, another new client shared with me that she'd just been diagnosed with a brain tumor, and in addition to working closely with her doctor, she wanted to increase her chances of recovery with positive food changes. We looked in this book and the recommendation was to reduce the consumption of meat, dairy, sugar, processed foods, soda, and caffeine, and increase the consumption of whole grains, organic vegetables, leafy greens, beans, sea vegetables, and water.

She dutifully came to our sessions, our group cooking classes, our visualization and affirmations workshops and increased her yoga and meditation practice.

Within months, she giddily shared with me that her brain tumor had vanished, likely with the course of action her doctor had given her, and perhaps also because of the shifts she made with her food and lifestyle choices. Her doctor had been surprised by how quickly the brain tumor had shrunk.

It dawned on me that a pattern was emerging here.

As I flipped through the book, apart from some very specific recommendations that pertained to the particular health concern, *practically every entry in the natural food healing book recommended the same thing*, as you can now guess: reducing the consumption of meat, dairy, sugar, processed foods, soda, and caffeine, and increasing the consumption of whole grains, organic vegetables, leafy greens, beans, sea vegetables, and water.

Coincidence? Probably not.

I began to see a pattern (in life and business) and noticed that just about everything could be improved with a particular set of "remedies," a system of *common denominator steps* that would create results for most everyone. I applied this "reliable results process" in my holistic nutrition business, with great success, even for people who simply wanted to shed those last five extra pounds.

Having this reliable results process allowed me to start thinking and moving beyond solely providing customized solutions for individuals and into also offering more leveraged group programs that were also more affordable for my clients because they didn't involve as much one-on-one time with me.

It wasn't until I started my first company, now called Boldheart. com (the parent company of our many programs, originally called ClientAttraction.com), that I saw the same thing happen again.

I had discovered as a result of my own experience in filling my first two practices, and in witnessing hundreds of my clients' success stories, that practically every business owner could attract a consistent stream of new clients by understanding 1) what interests their ideal client, 2) what their major struggles are, and 3) what will make them buy their services.

After just one year of working with dozens of individual clients, I noticed a consistent pattern. All my clients, without exception, needed to master the following steps to attract and sign on ideal, high-paying clients:

1. Make client attraction a priority.
2. Strategize their unique positioning in the marketplace.
3. Craft their ideal client profile.
4. Construct their compelling marketing message.
5. Package what they know, offer and charge.
6. Create pull-marketing materials.
7. Get out there in a big way.
8. Create their marketing action plan.
9. Become a master of closing the sale.
10. Implement systems for consistent action and results.

That's when my Proprietary System, The Client Attraction System®, was born and it helped hundreds of my clients get tremendous results from our private coaching.

What I never imagined in the beginning of creating this Proprietary System is that it would eventually allow me to go from working solely with one-to-one clients, to then working with small groups over the telephone, to creating home study products that generated multiple Six Figures a year, to teaching the system during three-day workshops with hundreds of attendees at each workshop. The system also solidified my reputation as a respected business mentor.

In the end, it became the bones of a complete education for business owners working toward making their first 10K a month consistently, which then morphed into the marketing process we now teach in our initial program, before a business owner is ready to leverage.

The process of leveraging one's business that I'm describing in this book (and what is now the Leveraged Business program) was created in the exact same way: based on unending research and experimentation, and documenting the process by which I leveraged my own business to Seven Figures, while gaining my life back. This Reliable Results Process is made up of the Eight Activators within the program (a taste of which is now in this book).

The program has since helped hundreds of entrepreneurs at the Leverage level to confidently turn their yearly revenues into their monthly revenues, while gaining their life back and being able to spend more time with their children or traveling.

That being said, your own Proprietary System, once documented and put in place, replaces the need for extreme customization. *It is about documenting the common denominators needed for success* and shifting your business model to provide that. It has the potential for reliably predicting positive future results for anyone who follows it, while allowing you to leverage your business even further because it can be duplicated or handled by others. This is leverage and it works across all industries.

The solution for cloning your (formerly intuitive) process is to examine every client case study you have worked with, and look for the pattern (formula) you used with the client to reach their desired goal. If you look closely enough, you will notice the similarities and common denominators.

The next step is to document these common actions into a process, step by step, in chronological order. We're talking about getting the *essence* of what works across the board for all clients, without the customized part, and putting it down on paper.

We look at *Content* (the steps), *Context* (the delivery) and *Culture* (the experience clients receive) to create the reliable results clients will get every time. By nailing these down, you'll begin to see a very distinctive pattern that will emerge.

NOTE: There is an important distinction between this Reliable Results Process (Content, Context, and Culture) vs. your Operations Manual (administrative procedures). This process is the documentation of the steps through which you currently take your clients so they create the results they're currently experiencing with you. It's the answer to the question, *"What must my clients and customers learn, do or experience to get positive results, in a predictable, reliable way?"*

Your process must be (practically) guaranteed to work. Even in the early days of my first coaching business, I knew in my heart that, if someone followed all the steps to my proprietary system (the ten steps I laid out above), they would get new clients consistently. To me, it was impossible not to, if you trusted the process and followed the formula in earnest. I believed in its efficacy so much that one of my early taglines became, *"More clients, in record time, guaranteed."*

Having a money-back guarantee attracted a lot of attention at networking events and on the speaking circuit, primarily because I believe that business owners are often skeptical of anyone who says that they can help you increase your results very quickly. But when I offered a guarantee along the lines of, *"Try this and if it doesn't work, you will get your money back,"* they became very intrigued and many hired me.

I didn't want to attract tire kickers, chronic skeptics or whiners who wouldn't be willing to do the work. So, mine was a *conditional guarantee*, meaning, to be eligible for the money-back guarantee if it didn't work, they would have to apply all the steps, fill out all the worksheets provided, complete all the assignments, follow the instructions, etc. If they did this and *didn't* get more clients, I would refund their coaching investment in full. The people who hired me agreed that this was fair.

Despite offering a conditional money-back guarantee, I was very nervous at first. I was wary of being taken advantage of, probably just as much as the clients originally were wary of investing in their business growth. There was a silver lining to this slight discomfort on my part. I had to create a Client Attraction System that was truly foolproof, that worked every time. Not only was my name on it, but now there was a money-back guarantee.

The money-back guarantee offer pushed me to further improve my system to create a verifiable, repeatable process that gave my clients (practically) guaranteed results. It had to work or my business was on the line. And so the more I learned and experimented with new strategies for attracting ideal clients in my own business, the more I tweaked the program to make it even better.

Whenever I found a new way to improve the closing of the sale process, I immediately added it to the scripts my private clients received. When I believed that having access to the recordings of our coaching calls helped my clients implement better, I added this as a bonus to my offerings. When I understood that daily accountability increased my clients' results, I implemented systems and practices to make the program even better, without charging more.

When I realized how much better their results were once I incorporated mindset teachings, I wove those into all of our processes in the program.

Although we are past the days of getting the attention of business owners by offering a money-back guarantee, we have kept tweaking our system for over twenty years to continually make the process better (and we still do.) This has allowed the process to morph into a Reliable Results Process for our clients, without the need for extreme customization. Because of this, now other people can teach this trusted process, other coaches coach our members, and content delivery can be automated.

Even though you may not have a business coaching company, the same can be true for you.

Consistency and reliability is scalable, whereby customized solutions aren't. When you build your Reliable Results Process so that your clients' results can be (practically) guaranteed, then you will be able to systematize, automate, or outsource your process into a more leveraged business model than you have now.

---

4. Your new scalable business model already exists, elsewhere.

Look up the ladder. When presented with the opportunity to switch their business model into one that will reduce the business owner's time, involvement and access, many entrepreneurs feel overwhelmed at the thought of reinventing how they deliver their products or services. They don't know where to start, don't see how they could pull it off, feel it can't be done in their industry and, frankly, they often draw a blank as to how to even go about it.

No need to worry or start from scratch!

The business model you seek, one that is truly leveraged and allows you to work with ten times the number of clients and customers (or more), already exists, either in your industry, a similar industry, or in a completely different realm of business. All you have to do is look for it.

If you come from the mindset that *someone else*, in another company much bigger than yours, has already leveraged their business to the level you'd like to someday reach, all it takes is some fact finding, asking around, and seeing what other people are doing.

(Incidentally, this is why successful business owners choose to mastermind with *other* highly successful business owners year after year. What works in one type of business can often be duplicated in another industry or a totally different type of business. Napoleon

Hill wrote about this in *Think and Grow Rich,* in the "Masterminding" chapter: in a collaborative model like this, *everyone learns from the collective wisdom of the group.)*

This act of seeing what already exists, what we call *Looking Up The Entrepreneurial Ladder™,* is a kind of fact-finding mission that starts with a simple question:

If you were to look up an imaginary ladder in your industry, bypass any individual or company that is doing "somewhat better" than you (we can use revenues or earnings, or even reach, if that's an easy benchmark), and go even further up the ladder to those doing ten times what you're producing, who is there?

To see a bigger future for yourself and actually believe that it can be done, the following questions will help you shift your mindset:

1) Who else does what you do in your field, but ten times bigger? (This might be in your industry or another, similar industry.)

2) What things do they do better?

3) What do they provide their clients/customers that you don't?

4) How are they positioned in your/their marketplace?

5) Who do they target as clients or customers? What kind of marketing angle do they use? Where do they advertise? What media do they use?

6) How much do they charge?

7) Finally, how exactly do they deliver their work in a leveraged way? How does this compare to the way you're delivering your work?

If they're doing as much as ten times what your company is doing a) they are likely onto something you don't know about yet, and b) they've proven that it can be done. There is "proof of concept" here. This means that, if they can do it in your industry or another similar one, *you can too.*

This type of inquiry works.

The business owners who have transformed their businesses by doing this exercise over the course of two days are the ones who cross the seven-figure mark. They appreciate the process of inquiry that comes out of pulling themselves out of their day-to-day operations and entering a new environment where they can safely ask themselves these questions, and discuss their answers with other growth-minded entrepreneurs, without fear of judgment.

The questions above give them an opportunity to see a bigger future for themselves than they have previously seen and help them tremendously in achieving forward motion.

An interior designer who was hovering for many years in the low Six Figures looked up the ladder and saw a national interior design firm with higher level clients, bigger projects, higher fees, more junior designers actually doing the work, higher-level marketing and social media, storefronts, product lines, etc. It pulled her out of her existing "rut" and into thinking and acting much bigger in her business.

She now had a new, much more affluent target audience, new marketing, new skill level, a new brand and website, and so on. She knew what to target because it first became possible for her in her mind's eye. Within two short years, she was well on her way to Seven Figures because she now had a path to model. She now has a million-dollar business because of this strategy and the direction she received.

It works in all industries. The same process has happened with a salon owner, an executive coach, a dental hygiene consulting practice, a professional organizer, functional medicine practitioners and chiropractors, a website designer, an online marketer, a relationship expert, and hundreds of others. It's a process that works, again and again.

So, who's ahead of you on your own Entrepreneurial Ladder™?

(Please understand that this exercise certainly isn't about *copying* what someone else is already doing, especially someone in your industry. That's not something you can do with integrity. Rather, it's about getting inspired, breaking that self-imposed ceiling by stretching your mindset around what's possible for you, modeling certain aspects of what's working for someone else, while doing things in your own way, one that is representative of your brand and essence.)

There's no need to rip off the Band-Aid that quickly. After looking up this proverbial ladder, it can become confusing, and, frankly, *terrifying* to go from one business model (the current one that pays all the bills) to an unknown one. The saying, *"The devil you know is better than the devil you don't know"* is alive and well when making this kind of change and can accurately describe how many entrepreneurs feel.

There is a sense of worry that, if they release the one trapeze rung they're used to holding onto then grasp the other (presumably bigger) one, they will fall and lose all they've built so far.

That's not what we're suggesting. You don't need to pour all you've done so far down the drain. There is a lot to be said about successfully transitioning from one business model to another, with an emphasis on the word *transition*.

A hybrid business model can be a good transition point, whereby you continue to do some elements of what you deliver the same way you have for years, while adding new elements that will begin to remove you from the delivery, or to work with groups, or even to bring on associates, allowing you to work with many more people.

This transition period in shifting business models allows you, for a short period of time or even a year or two, to keep one hand on the original trapeze rung and grasp the other as well, at least until the confidence and proof of concept is there.

Some of our members have done just this. Instead of moving directly from doing one-to-one work onsite with executives in corporations, to working only with *groups* of executives at the coach's location, they instead created a hybrid business model. They still worked *privately* with their original clients, but also added access to a pre-recorded (common denominator) curriculum that could be consumed online by not just this one client, but all clients. They also added additional coaches to work with the executive's team.

Hybrid business models can look like this (or a combination of these):

- private work + online curriculum + group Q&A calls
- private work + group sessions + private forum
- private work + associates stepping in to help out and add more value
- private work + a three-day event for all clients at once

This hybrid option gave them the ability to keep offering "private work" but also to begin transitioning to leveraged business solutions beyond the hours-for-dollars business model. If you look at what's up your Entrepreneurial Ladder and what your current business model is, what's the bridge?

You too can start there, before taking the full leap. Just don't get too comfortable in this "transition" place. We eventually want to move you to a fully leveraged business model, so you can work with more people, while getting your freedom back.

5. New Level, New Devil.

Resistance is simply The Big Breakdown Before the Big Breakthrough. The resistance you may experience when the idea of moving to the next level of business comes up is a rite of passage for many business owners. In fact, it's fairly predictable.

With the decision to move from a one-to-one business model into a more scalable one, fears will come up. When we help business owners multiply their revenues by shifting their delivery model, it's not unusual for a roomful of otherwise confident and successful adults to experience fears and hold on to beliefs about why *"It won't work for my business."*

Here are some of the fears we've regularly seen come up for entrepreneurs as they step into changing into a different, more leveraged business model:

Fear of being copied by competitors or by their own employees if the work goes online; fear that clients will no longer get results and leave; fear of losing control; fear of being embezzled, harassed, overwhelmed, publicly criticized, or humiliated; feeling inadequate or like they're not good enough to play at that level; worried they will lose their integrity, approachability, and authenticity once they get bigger; fear of feeling like a fraud or being found out for not having it all together, fear that it was all a "lucky streak" and not duplicatable; fear of failure; fear of overexposure from too much success; even fear of death, which is a surprise to all, etc.

As our entrepreneurs have admitted, many of these can feel irrational, but were nonetheless still present for them. These fears and beliefs are absolutely normal reactions, as I've experienced in my own entrepreneurial journey and from having witnessed thousands of business owners on their path to leverage.

We call each successive move up a "new level," and with each new level comes a new set of fears and general sense of resistance. In our program, we call this phenomenon:

"New Level, New Devil."

The closer an entrepreneur gets to breaking through to the next bigger level, the more fears and resistance will come up. Essentially, it's fear of change, one of the greatest paralyzing factors that keeps you from going bigger.

When the fear strikes, an energy of wanting to dig your heels into the ground and stop all forward movement appears. Instead of taking big actions toward the next level, you may find yourself self-sabotaging, questioning, waffling, being indecisive, wondering if you really want to move up, preferring instead the "devil you know," and staying in your comfort zone. And a great urge to go hide under the covers.

This has happened to me many times in my own business. In fact, it's now so predictable that I've come to expect it. So should you. Once you recognize it as Resistance and you understand that it's a mindset trick being played on you by your ego to keep you small and safe, you recognize it for being what we call *The Big Breakdown Before the Big Breakthrough.*

There are different types of breakdowns that I've seen "show up," primarily an urge to want to retreat in a big way, feeling, *"It's not worth it"* or *"I can't do this."*

Steven Pressfield, in his book The War of Art, writes, *"The danger is greatest when the finish line is in sight. At this point, Resistance knows we're about to beat it. It hits the panic button. It marshals one last assault and slams us with everything it's got . . . Be wary at the end."*

Thoughts of resistance will come up, such as:

- *"Who do you think you are, anyway?"*
- *"This isn't for you. You can't do this!"*
- *"Why do you have to be so greedy? Be happy with what you have!"*
- *"You don't have what it takes to do this."*
- *"You don't deserve to be that successful."*
- *"You'll never amount to anything, you never have, so why bother!"*

These thoughts can seemingly come out of nowhere, even for very successful people. Yes, they can feel debilitating, but they're not "real." They are just random thoughts going through your mind, things you picked up in childhood or as part of your culture that are now causing doubt, fear and worry, and essentially having you question whether it's safe to leave your comfort zone.

Do not underestimate this resistance. It is prevalent and can be debilitating to business growth.

So, how do you get past the resistance or as we call it, the "drunk monkey" thoughts polluting your mindset and sabotaging your forward motion? 1) observe the resistance, 2) be comfortable being uncomfortable, 3) understand that it really isn't valid, and that 4) it's just your old paradigm not yet having integrated with your new stretch goals.

Then, circle back around to the fact that your obligation (moral, divine or financial, as you prefer) to serve many more people is far more important than any fear or discomfort you may be experiencing in the short term. Each time you experience this resistance, recognize it for what it is and know that you are on the verge of a new bigger breakthrough. Then, celebrate. If you use this process, you will eventually move past the resistance and into big action.

Beware of Growth Guilt. Another big deterrent for some business owners in making the decision to change their business model and go for scalability comes in the form of guilt. *"I have so much already, why would I want more? Isn't this enough?"*

The following is a common scenario. Entrepreneurs often ask, *"How do you keep from feeling guilty when everything in your business is going well but people around you are going through a difficult time? What do I do when someone tells me how much they're struggling in their business, but then ask me how I am doing in mine? Part of me wants to hide my success so they don't feel bad about their own situation, but I work too hard at creating something amazing to diminish it."*

They admit to getting caught up in the idea that it's not noble or integrous to go beyond what they have, as though it were shameful to abandon the one-to-one business model and strive for more.

Beliefs come up around the idea that *expanding* means that we are *leaving "us little people" behind.*

Here are some fears we've heard many times:

Fear of being personally criticized and judged by friends and family (even colleagues and clients) for having "made it" while they're still struggling; fear of abandonment and disapproval from their community; fear of not belonging anymore because they broke the social stereotype; worrying that others (including family members) will now start knocking on their door for money and they won't be able to say no, etc.

This is what I've come to call *Growth Guilt,* and it stops business owners who seek expansion from actually taking the actions that would result in growth.

How does one get past Growth Guilt? Understand that your journey is yours, and theirs is their own. You do not owe anyone *anything*, any money, and certainly you do not owe anyone the act of staying small so as to not outshine them.

There's no need for you to feel guilty for wanting to create more impact in the world or being rewarded for it.

We *all* have the opportunity to stretch and do more. If your family, friends, business colleagues (or anyone else for whom you might be making yourself small) genuinely wanted to know how you got to where you are or achieve what you're attempting to achieve so they could attempt the same, *they would ask you.* That's what successful people do. They look at others who are doing well and say, *"How did you do it? What are you doing now that's working?"* and they model it or join them on the path.

Keep on doing what you're doing and being the best person you can be, without flaunting it or rubbing it in. It's tempting to want to have others in your life drink the proverbial Kool-Aid you've been drinking, but refrain until they ask. It can absolutely backfire on you and affect your relationships.

If they ask for advice, give it to them. If they don't, there's no need to offer it, or to feel guilty for your own willingness to do things differently. When they ask, "How's business?" and you feel that they're not actually interested in your answer, you can simply answer, "It pays the bills!" and then change the subject and ask about them.

Then, keep on going.

What's the impact of applying the Business Model Activator in your business? Michelle went from working as the only person delivering results in her business, to having an entire team of qualified consultants doing it in her proprietary way.

Michelle explains it to you in her own words:

"When I met Fabienne, I was in the place where I'd given myself a year to make my business work or I was going to shut it down. I was running my business on the side of my corporate job, and had only made about $4,000.

"Even though I was someone who'd been very skeptical about anyone trying to sell me anything, I trusted Fabienne. I work with corporations, but the models that are taught here work. What is true for B2C is absolutely applicable for B2B. So I rolled up my sleeves with my accountability partner (one of the best aspects of the Leveraged Business program is that you no longer need to figure this out on your own!) and made it work.

"In just two years, I've surpassed $500,000 in this business. But, what has been incredibly inspiring is watching others achieve and surpass their goals and knowing that this entire community has my back. I've seen others achieve greatness and then lovingly share how they did it. Which has meant I could do it too." —Michelle Tenzyk

Leverage Your Marketing

OBJECTIVE:

Use omnipresent marketing to bring in an unprecedented number of qualified leads, without you being the one involved in the day-to-day lead generation.

TO INCREASE your impact and get your revenues from Six Figures to Seven Figures usually requires a dramatic increase in the number of clients and customers you attract (and then sign on) to your business. To add another zero in this way then requires as little as a twofold and as much as a tenfold increase in lead-generation efforts.

This, in turn, means that the volume of your marketing activities needs to increase proportionally.

Admittedly, that seems like a lot of work for someone who's already maxed out and likely overwhelmed. But the good news is, you don't have to be the one to generate all of it yourself. It's time to leverage your existing marketing channels and add new ones, with a focus on creating *systems* and *repeatable processes* for everything, ones that ideally do not require more of you, and eventually, may not require you much at all.

1. You are a marketer *first*.

Your number one job, arguably the most important one you have, is to be the best and most prolific marketer you can be. At first, this may feel like a shock to you, and you wouldn't be the first. I have rarely met people who started their own business because they said, "I can't wait to spend a majority of my time marketing, leaving my comfort zone to get myself out there! Oh, how I wish I could spend more of my time doing what I love best, the marketing piece."

You probably didn't start your business saying this either. No, you, like the proverbial 99.9999 percent of business owners, got into your business likely because 1) you wanted freedom, instead of working for someone else; 2) you were good at something, and you wanted to do more of it, but on your terms; and 3) you wanted to make a difference in people's lives—a real impact.

I am willing to bet that you weren't giddily looking forward to doing the marketing piece. In fact, you probably didn't even realize how much marketing (and selling) you actually needed to do, thinking that clients and customers would just come to you, right? Or that it is arguably the most important job you have in the business, even more so than the actual "work" of delivering the promised services, results, or products.

You see, consistent and effective marketing is what runs the business, more so than the work you do, at least in the first few years. If you don't have a steady pipeline of new *prospects* coming in, you have no *clients*. And if you have no *clients*, there is no *money*.

And if there's no *money*, well, you don't have a business, you just have an *expensive hobby*.

    I have long taught a mindset shift to our program members, and it is that you are a marketer *first and foremost*, before anything else.

You are a marketer who provides insurance.

You are a marketer who consults.

You are a marketer who coaches.

You are a marketer who provides financial services.

You are a marketer who speaks from the stage.

You are a marketer who provides nutritional advice.

You are a marketer who cooks.

You are a marketer who teaches people how to make their homes beautiful.

You are a marketer who designs houses.

You are a marketer who helps people with their bookkeeping.

It is a rather tough concept to get your head around at first, especially because you probably didn't attend a two-year marketing school before opening your business. We celebrate those who build a better mousetrap, not those who market a better mousetrap. For you, as for many, marketing is a necessary task, and if you didn't have to do it, you would be perfectly happy.

The more marketing you do, the more you will reach the clients and customers divinely contracted to work with you. That said, how you feel about marketing dictates how much of it you do.

I deeply believe that marketing can be a divine tool. Just as rich people aren't evil (it's just evil people who are evil, and there are plenty of people without much money who are evil too), the same applies to marketing.

Marketing is like power; it can be used for good or for bad. You can decide on the type of marketer you want to be—sleazy, inauthentic, and dishonest, or:

- Authentic
- Loving
- Integrous
- Kind
- Generous

It really depends on you and how you wish to "do" marketing.

A few years ago, a woman came up to me at one of my three-day marketing workshops and said to me, "This better work because I hate marketing." I had heard this many times before and lovingly grabbed her hands. With compassion in my heart, I responded, "The only reason you hate marketing is because of how you feel about marketing itself. Once I teach you to feel differently about marketing, you will begin to love it, and then you will want to do it all the time. This will change your business forever."

She was skeptical, but I made her promise to come up to me at the end of the three days and let me know if there had been any development on this hatred for marketing.

At the end of the workshop she came up to me with tears of gratitude in her eyes and said, "You were absolutely right. Now that I see it through your lens of divinity, I love marketing. I actually can't wait to get home and put myself and my message out there in a much bigger way. Thank you."

Can you really transform your relationship with marketing that quickly? Yes. It just takes a shift in perspective, from thinking of marketing as something you do *to* someone, to thinking of it as something you do *for* someone.

Okay, so what shifted for her, specifically?

She began to look beyond the burden of her everyday marketing tasks and instead at the big picture of her life's purpose. And then she looked at the role of marketing itself in helping her activate her greater purpose.

When you can somehow connect the role of marketing as the amplifier of your message and of your life's purpose (or the purpose of your business), you slowly begin to embrace this new role of yours, that of being a marketer first.

This is when everything changes for the better. You begin to shift your energy around this marketing *thing*, put more focus on it, learn to systematize it, and put it to good use. It becomes a reliable friend you can always count on, in good times and in bad.

The more you make marketing your priority, the more prospects come your way, the more your pipeline is continually full of people listening to your message, some of whom will eventually become your clients or customers. This means that more money comes into the business, which also means that you can afford a better and larger team. This then leads to you being able to document your processes and methodologies, so that the team can begin to take over some of the daily tasks that previously kept you in the role of "bottleneck" in the company.

And because you begin seeing real results from your new focus on marketing, after a while, you begin to actually love marketing.

Never ever take your finger completely off the pulse of the marketing controls. Because many business owners don't initially *love* marketing, there is often a propensity to 1) not do it, or 2) completely abdicate it—meaning you hurry to get someone else to do the "dirty work" of the marketing strategy for you, so you never have to think about it again.

The problem is, marketing is one of (if not *the*) most important aspects of your business, and it still requires you to some extent. Even if you eventually hire a marketing director or a marketing manager, you must *still* be involved in this aspect of the business, until the very last day.

You might say, "But I thought I was supposed to delegate all the things I don't like or am not good at. Now you're telling me I must still do this thing I'm only somewhat competent at?"

Yes. This is the one exception, at least at this stage of your business. The idea around leveraging your business is to get as many things off your plate as humanly possible. That is, except for your marketing and sales *strategy*. The strategy is something you must always attend to, even if you're not fully driving it or you get lots of help with it.

Here's what I mean and why it's important. Your business has a *soul*, and that soul within your business is held by you. When you're present, and you are involved in the marketing (at least the strategy, angle, and essence of it) people resonate with the essence that is *you*. It's hard to explain but they, well, feel you are part of the business.

Conversely, when you've completely abdicated the marketing strategy and the "voice" in the marketing copy, or when someone else is doing your videos and all of your social media posts for you, the result can feel canned and lifeless—Elvis has left the building. This isn't going to create a movement. Don't worry, though. I'm not suggesting you do *all* of the marketing. Just the *high-level driving* of the marketing.

As the business owner, you must be a part of every big marketing decision and the overall message, and make sure these are congruent with what you stand for and whom you're talking to (remember, no outside person will likely know your clients or customers the way you do). Then you can step to the side and have *someone else* execute on the marketing directives for you.

2. Your goal is to be omnipresent.

Stop keeping yourself and your company a secret. One of the best compliments I received early in my entrepreneurial career happened at a business networking group in New York. As I walked in and scanned the room to see if there was anyone I knew, a man turned to me and exclaimed, "My God, you're everywhere!" and I laughed and said, "Thank you!" Apparently, he'd seen me at several other networking groups over the previous two weeks. The following week, he hired me to help him grow his business.

This happened again a few years ago, when a joint venture partner approached me about doing a strategic alliance. We had just started a Skype session and before diving in, I asked her how she had found out about me and my business. She responded, "How could I not? Everywhere I turn, there you are, Fabienne. It's like you're on surround sound in my life!"

Yet again, a week ago, a brand-new member of our program and I were beginning an initial strategy call and I asked, "What made you decide to enroll in the program and work with me?" and she replied, "I've been following you for about a year, and was thinking it might be time to work with you, and lo and behold, I received your letter in the mail, right after getting a lovely phone call from one of your team members. The next day, I saw you pop up on Facebook. It was a sign that *now* was the time I should work with you."

I have countless stories like this and, although it feels synchronistic, even divinely led on the receiving end—which it may very well be—it is also not accidental. It is the end result of *consistency* and what I call Marketing Omnipresence.

Omnipresence can be loosely translated as "being present everywhere at all times, at the same time" or "to appear everywhere simultaneously." When applied to marketing, it is the kind of exponential leverage that is missing from most people's marketing plans.

Imagine that your marketing message, your company name, your brand and offers, could be seen by your ideal prospects practically everywhere they turned. What would happen to your sales and your revenues? My guess is that more people would work with you and that it would drive growth.

Shooting for omnipresence means taking every opportunity to surround your prospects with, well, *you*. Or your message. This requires looking at all the places your prospects "hang out" and then being present there, in full force, in a variety of different channels, with valuable content and useful information.

If you don't have ten times the number of clients or customers you want, the problem is likely *not* that you're not good at what you do. No, your only "problem" may be a combination of *obscurity* and *anonymity*. The solution requires that, from this day forward, you make the commitment and constant effort to be out there in the world (well, at least in your prospects' world) in a much bigger way than you are now, and let them know you exist.

If you or your company are currently reaching 10,000 people through all your channels and social media, the mindset shift that needs to happen is to focus on creating visibility to 20,000, and then eventually 100,000 or 1,000,000 of your prospects (or more) as your goal each year. It's about dramatically adding *quantity* to your *quality*, and to stop the tendency of wanting to hide behind your computer or avoid marketing altogether.

It's a commitment to leveraging your marketing so that you can reach more of the people who desperately need you but don't know you exist.

Omnipresence in marketing allows you to fast track your expert status and be seen as the authority in your field. When a prospect looks for information about your topic and many of the useful bits of information they find have been created by you, you become their trusted source. This will considerably increase your credibility in their eyes and it paves the way for a much easier sale once they raise their hand.

Think blogging, free reports, online summits, webinars, free assessments, quizzes, articles, podcasts, free templates, checklists, a mobile app, books, lead-generating (online) ads like Google Ads and Facebook Ads, high-content videos, extensive social media presence, being a contributing author to publications or sites that cater specifically to your target audience, in your particular niche, speaking, sponsorship, booths at trade shows, etc.

We're looking for (small) market dominance here. This is about you being the big fish in a small fishbowl, the first person someone thinks about when they talk about your industry.

You can manufacture what your prospects see as "a sign" to work with you. Have you ever been recommended a book three different times from three different people, and upon hearing about it the third time, you finally said, "Wow, it's a sign, I need to get that book and read it"?

I know that if I am experiencing a particular challenge in my personal life or in my business and the same solution to this problem shows up from different sources (a friend tells me about a particular consultant; a business colleague recommends a book written by the founder of that same company; and a Facebook ad pops up inviting me to a webinar from, again, that same consultant), because I don't believe in coincidences, I am going to start paying very close attention to this said consultant.

I will likely read the person's book, sign up for that person's email newsletter, maybe check out her videos on YouTube, sign up for a webinar, maybe even read her testimonials on the website. I would become very curious and want to find out more about how I can work with that person.

Then, if I get a call from her customer service team asking if I wanted to explore working together or if I received a letter with an outstanding client testimonial, maybe with a call to action to work with them, the odds are heavily stacked that I will likely work with that person. It's as if they've been on surround sound in my own life and will begin to be very top of mind for me, feeling as if all these mentions were serendipitous, a lucky and unexpected sign, as if it is *meant to be* that I should work with her. And it likely is.

Now, if we put our business owner/marketer hats on, we understand that this type of omnipresence isn't just a *coincidence* but rather a choreographed series of marketing touches. It is the sort of "serendipity" that comes from a company (yours) knowing exactly *who* your clients are, what their biggest *struggles* tend to be and exactly what's going to get them the *result* they so badly want and help them to reach their highest aspirations.

And then, being committed to leverage your existing marketing efforts to lovingly surround them with content, solutions, social proof and calls to action, everywhere they turn, in a variety of channels with great frequency, so they see you in at least three places and consistently. Imagine that your solution kept showing up in their life (with authenticity, compassion, integrity, and a loving message) just at the right time, from different sources, again and again. Would they consider working with you?

Yes, probably, and with much greater frequency than is happening for you now. The key for it to feel right is not to be *aggressive* but rather, *lovingly omnipresent*.

The mindset shift I invite you to make as it relates to your marketing is that it's YOUR job to be ever-present in your prospects' lives and that you must show up in different channels, so that you literally, and systematically appear to be everywhere. The importance is to embrace the idea of seeming like you are in surround sound in their life and that working with you is the logical choice they look forward to making. When done with the right energy (pulling vs. pushing hard), this feels nice on their end, as well as yours.

Be the biggest fish in a small pond. One of my serial clients over the years, Kate, found me through a listing for a seminar I was doing in New York City close to fifteen years ago. Even though she never ended up attending my "How to attract all the clients you need" evening seminar, she looked me up and found me online and called me to set up a Get Acquainted Call. After a brief conversation, she quickly signed up to work with me.

Kate was an out-of-work actor who had taken a job as a receptionist to make ends meet in between gigs. Being high-energy and someone who loves to add value anywhere she can, she offered to place outbound prospecting calls for the owner of the company to help set up meetings with prospects. Essentially, she was cold calling for her employer and it was working.

The owner was delighted that she had this uncanny ability to schedule meetings for him with usually difficult-to-reach C-suite corporate prospects, whereby his other staff members weren't able to do this. She loved doing it, became very good at scheduling these sales calls and eventually decided to leave her job to open up her own business teaching other companies how to get their sales teams to successfully set up more sales meetings with prospects by using her cold calling system and unique process.

The problem was, she didn't have a client. So, she hired me, and I taught her how to do a few things to get clients. Right away, she landed a copier-dealer company as her first client. She was thrilled, especially since the sales team started experiencing an unprecedented spike in new meetings scheduled with C-level prospects.

Within four months of us working together, she was making $10,000 a month. Soon, she asked me, "Okay, Fabienne, what's next? What other types of clients should I go for?"

My answer: "You don't."

"Kate, you are crushing your results with this type of business technology client. Instead of going for another industry altogether, let's use the existing success with this one type of client, and reach out to other copier-dealers in New York and say, 'Hey, if I can do this for your competitor, I can also do this for you. Are you interested in hearing more?'"

At first, she cold called (of course), pitched and eventually worked with the majority of the New York business technology dealers. She closed one, then another, and then another. Word spread within the New York business technology niche. It was as if she had become the Business Technology Sales Whisperer.

Referrals eventually came in for her to do business with regional sales teams, and based on our marketing coaching, she increased the *minimum* size of the sales groups she would work with from three to twenty-five. This allowed her to get paid more as she was paid by the number of delegates. She was using the same amount of time, but leveraging that time by working with many more people, thereby making more.

It continued to work. We knew we were onto something, so we decided to go further with this.

I told her, "Kate, let's go vertical with this industry and have you saturate and own all things related to cold-calling within the business technology space. Let's have you be omnipresent so every-where they turn, they only hear about you. Let's focus on signing up all other copier-dealers in New York and then regionally, and ultimately, nationally. Let's have you be *the biggest fish in the pond* so they are no longer interested in working with anyone but you, meaning, you are the only logical choice in their eyes. Let's shoot for omnipresence."

That's when I could hear her smile over the phone. She knew she could do it.

Eventually, the large national and international companies got wind of Kate and started asking her to come speak at their annual conferences and hired her for their national sales trainings.

And that's exactly what took Kate from $0 to five figures a month, to Six Figures within one year, and toward ultimately making more than $80,000 a month (Seven Figures a year) within a few short years, with very low overhead. She had learned to leverage her marketing by saturating *one very specific niche* and becoming a superstar within this niche.

The same thing happened recently to Terri, a practice manage-ment consultant for oral surgery clients. Terri had a low six figure consulting practice when she joined the program. I shared Kate's story with Terri and we went about dramatically increasing her visibility in the oral surgery field, rather than expanding too quickly into the general dentistry field.

As you can imagine, everyone knows everyone in a niched field such as oral and maxillofacial surgery. When one surgeon told another about the results he'd gotten from working with Terri's company, she was easily hired. And this happened again and again.

But to greatly expand her reach, visibility and exposure, we didn't just depend on word of mouth. She focused on becoming omnipresent in this niche with regular email marketing, speaking at all the annual oral surgery conferences, contributing to an important book in the industry, producing direct-mail campaigns, and more, with a focus on being known by all as the ultimate expert in her field.

And this strategy worked.

People now come up to her at conferences and they *know* about her; they talk about her on the bathroom line not even knowing that she can overhear them. To Terri, this is funny because she has always been more introverted, not really a seeker of the spotlight, and generally not one you would consider to fit the traditional "rock star" archetype. But that's who she's become, because she leveraged her marketing to focus on saturating one particular industry, becoming the big fish in a relatively small pond.

And that's how Terri went from making just over $100K in her business, to a million a year in revenues, just thirty-six months later. Oh, and going from almost no vacation to six weeks of vacation per year. To be inspired, you can read Terri's full story (and watch her video account of this) at **www.TheLeveragedBusiness.com**.

For you to experience similar results in your own business, I recommend shifting your mindset so that you avoid being *all things* to *all people*. Trying to appeal to many niches at once can be rather expensive and very time-consuming. Instead, the riches are in the niches, where you commit to leveraging your marketing so that you dominate a single niche, like Kate and Terri have done so successfully.

---

3. Crank up the volume on your marketing, more than you think.

You control how much you make, simply by how much you're *willing* to market. Would you like to go from Six Figures to Seven Figures (or more) in your business? The process is simple, actually. Now that you're thinking of leveraging your business model to accommodate ten times more clients or customers, it's time to increase your marketing by ten times too. (It can sound time consuming and overwhelming at first, but stay with me, as it doesn't have to be.)

I have long believed that how much you make is absolutely within your control, *and no one else's*, at least when you're self-employed or own a business. Over the course of my work with entrepreneurs at every stage of business, one of the most common questions I've gotten is, "Fabienne, how much marketing do I *really* need to do to grow my client base significantly? I've got so much to do as it is, how little marketing can I get away with?"

Well, it's really about simple *math* first, then *willingness*, followed by *commitment*.

So first, let's start with the math part:

As in the *Leverage Your Accountability* Activator, we've got to get clear on what your target is. Let's pick a basic formula, just to keep it simple. Let's say that, by this time next year, you want to have ten times the number of clients or customers you have now. (I know, big stretch, but we're just playing here, just to stretch your mindset and get you thinking so much bigger. Remember, it always starts with stretching your *mindset around what's possible*. Once that happens, everything follows seamlessly.)

Ok, so for argument's sake, let's say you have ten clients now. Multiplying this by ten would make a goal target of one hundred clients or customers within twelve months. (Yes, in your particular industry and depending on how long clients stay or leave, there may be some clients who roll off or transition away from working with you, but let's keep this really simple, just for this exercise.)

10 x 10 current clients = 100 new clients in 12 months

First, how many new clients would you need to add per month?

You get to this number by dividing the number one hundred (that's how many new clients you want) by twelve. A hundred new clients over the course of twelve months is an average of signing on a little over eight new clients a month.

100 new clients ÷ 12 months =
approximately 8 new clients per month

Next, looking back and "guesstimating" how often you close the sale when talking to each prospect, what's that percentage? For every ten sales conversations you've had over the last month, how many did you close? Half? Then that means you have an average of a 50 percent conversion rate. If you close two out of ten, then that's 20 percent.

10 sales calls ÷ 5 sales closed = 50% conversion rate

Let's say it's 50 percent, just to make the math easy. That means that, if you need to close an average of eight new clients per month, you will need to have a minimum of sixteen "sales conversations" per month.

8 new clients x 50% conversion rate = 16 sales calls per month

So, to stay with this exercise, let's say that you need to have "x-number" of sales conversations per month to reach your year-end target. Based on the numbers you worked out so far, how many qualified prospects do you need to have a sales conversation with every month? (In our sample exercise, the number is sixteen. What's your actual number, based on how many new clients you want to sign on per month?) Are you having that many sales conversations (what we call "Get Acquainted Calls") now each month?

Based on this, do you suppose you would have to do *more* marketing than you're doing now? (The answer is likely yes.) If so, how much more marketing? Two times? Five times?

Let's just get real, here.

If you're not much of a math enthusiast (and let's be frank, it's not unusual for a business owner to be minutiae-challenged), you can just forget all of this and boil it down to the following sentence that I invite you to now embrace:

"I am ready to market a lot more than I'm marketing now, about ten times more. It's time for me to seriously turn up the volume on my exposure, visibility, marketing sequences and follow-up."

It's really about you becoming a marketer first, and committing to increasing your marketing activities dramatically, remembering that the only type of marketing we're committed to doing is with authenticity, integrity and love.

Okay, so that was the *math* aspect. Now, we move onto the *willingness* part.

Remember the example about providing the cure for cancer we talked about earlier? This is about the *willingness* to become that person who wants to impact more people, either within your community, or within the world at large.

There is a litmus test that I'm fond of, to check your willingness factor. It has to do with how hungry you are to get new results. As it relates to your *willingness* to market in a big way, ask yourself which of these statements best describes you right now:

1) "I could eat."

2) "I'm hungry."

3) "I am *famished*, starving, ready to do just about anything (with integrity, of course) and get out there so that my people can find me. I am willing to do whatever it takes to reach my goal of increasing my reach by a factor of ten (or two)! *Watch me do it!*"

Whichever statement you chose will likely explain your current results. If you understand that your next several hundred clients or next few thousand customers are literally in pain or experiencing anxiety, discomfort, depression or any other emotion because they don't have a solution to their biggest problem, but that *you do*, it becomes a real motivation to get out there and let the world know that you exist.

That said, they won't find you automatically or by accident. You must be willing to market in a much bigger way and let them know that you exist. Conversely, if you keep hiding your services and making yourself a secret, you can't help as many people.

I invite you to shift your mindset to be fully willing to put your own needs, wants or energy level aside; to move beyond the "I could eat" stage, and go for "I'm hungry," or better yet, "I am famished and will do whatever it takes."

And finally, the *commitment* part.

This is about taking personal responsibility and becoming a disciplined marketer. Learning what works from those already getting results, and then doing that and only that. Getting help. Understanding that marketing is one of the most important things you can do. Putting it above all else. Understanding that, as visionary and chief business development officer, it's your role to do all you can to reach those who (perhaps) desperately need your company's services or products.

It's about eliminating the excuses, and becoming really *committed*.

My good friend John Assaraf, multimillionaire many times over, respected marketer and best-selling author, shared a quote with me on the phone many years ago that I've never forgotten. He said, "Fabienne, when you're *interested*, you do what's *convenient*. When you're *committed*, you do *whatever it takes*."

Hearing these words sent chills down my spine back then. It was as if he'd distilled into a few words what I believed all along about life and business. You must be *committed* to see exponential results.

Turn up the volume on what's *already* working for you. Okay, but ramping up the volume on your marketing can feel very overwhelming, especially when we're talking about a ten times increase, and even more so when you're already overwhelmed. Rest assured. I'm not necessarily talking about finding new-fangled ways of getting the word out there and creating complexity by learning lots of new marketing techniques, although that helps. We're not there yet.

First, let's start with the marketing activities that are already working for you, those already getting results, and let's turn up the volume on those activities. Here's the marketing pie we share with all members in our program, to help you figure out what you're already doing, and where you could do more:

YOUR MARKETING PIE™

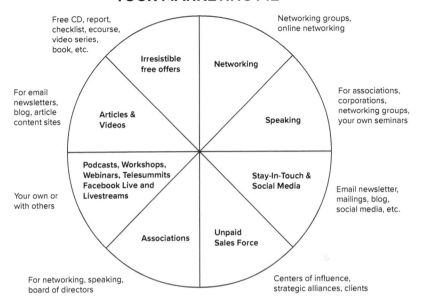

Are you currently getting most of your new business from word-of-mouth, but not doing much to generate it? Create systems for generating referrals from existing clients, referral sources and strategic alliances, so that you're doing something to generate lots of referrals at least once a month (ten to twelve times per year).

Are you a natural "influencer," comfortable speaking from the stage, but you only speak in public once or twice a year? Start speaking twice a month, anywhere they'll have you; get comfortable doing video and produce a video a week that you post to your YouTube channel and other viral video distribution sites; host livestreams or Facebook Lives on a weekly basis; get booked to speak at all your industry's annual conferences, as Terri and Kate did.

Are friendships and building trusting relationships your strong suit, but you only network and meet new people in a business setting once or twice a year? Join three to four new networking groups, and especially ones that meet weekly so that you're networking with other referral partners and business owners at least eight to ten times a month.

Are you incredibly knowledgeable about your topic or industry, but also painfully shy? Perhaps writing is your strong suit instead. Begin writing prolifically, several times per week. Write materials such as thought leader articles, blog posts, special reports, quizzes and assessments; write a direct-mail letter to prospects once a month; become a contributing author to several publications, groups or websites that have already gathered your ideal clients; write a short, lead-generating, high-content and high-value book that you plan to give away for free on your website (our members learn how to write a book in as little as ninety days), and invite readers to work with you.

Everyone is wired differently and has different skills and strengths. The key is to begin by harnessing *what's already working for you* and then *multiply your efforts in that marketing activity*. This, in turn, brings in a lot more leads and prospects, and eventually clients. It's simple math. Then, you can always add more marketing channels, so you end up on surround sound in your prospects' lives.

Admittedly, this can seem overwhelming when your time is already maxed out. Don't worry, this won't all depend on you, as we'll create systems for marketing more without you being as involved in the marketing implementation as you may have been in the past.

---

4. The money is in you consistently being in touch.

Systematize your follow-up (and never call it "follow-up").
In working with so many entrepreneurs over the years, I have noticed that there are often "money-on-the-table opportunities" that business owners don't take advantage of, to the tune of tens of

thousands of dollars waiting to be cashed in on. They're looking for increased cash flow, and the potential money is there, but they don't always see it, until it's pointed out to them.

One of those "money-on-the-table opportunities" is almost always in the follow-up process. The leads already exist, in one of the following forms:

- people who have expressed interest in what you offer
- people who have raised their hand to find out more about working with you, but were never taken through the closing-of-the-sale process
- referrals who were never contacted
- past prospects who didn't sign up at the time
- even past clients or customers who are not being contacted regularly about working together again

Why haven't they been closed?

Well, let's face it. Following up with prospects on a regular basis, until they become clients, doesn't always happen consistently. This is because it currently requires *you* and there is likely no more of *you* to go around, so the follow-up often falls through the cracks. (Plus, the concept of following up isn't always as appealing as that of meeting new people.)

Here's the deal, though. These unclosed prospects are, other than being lovely human beings, money-on-the-table opportunities. Some of the marketing has already been done to introduce them to you and now it's time to market to them until they're ready to sign up to work with you.

Now, if you understand the age-old marketing concept that an individual must see your marketing message seven to nine times before they consider buying or hiring you, I ask you this:

Have you been in touch with your prospects by phone or email seven to nine times over the course of the last few months?

The answer is likely no. Why? Again, in most cases, this is because it requires you to do the following up and nurturing aspect required to turn a lead into a prospect, and a prospect into a client and four things are currently getting in the way of you doing so:

1) You don't have the time to follow up.
2) There are too many of them to follow up with.
3) You don't want to be a pest or bother them.
4) You're (likely) not wired as someone who loves to follow up consistently, systematically, on a certain day each week or each month, for years to come.

And yes, these are all absolutely valid "reasons" for not staying in touch, which is why most busy business owners don't follow up and eventually let their leads go from warm to cold. Sadly, those leads get forgotten and these leads also eventually forget you.

They simply haven't been contacted enough to have become clients or customers. That being said, if they *had* been followed up with systematically, a certain (perhaps large) percentage would have gladly hired you or worked with your company.

So, what do you do if you don't have the time or aren't wired to follow up consistently? To fully leverage your marketing, it's time to *systematize* your follow-up. As I did in the Leverage Your Systems Activator, I invite you now to start thinking about *systematizing* your marketing too, so that when your marketing systems are running smoothly, these processes can liberate you from being the one who does everything. Having marketing systems in place will help you clone or replace yourself in the follow-up process.

This involves using a stay-in-touch marketing process (a sequence or a funnel, as it's called) to follow up on leads so that you appear to consistently be in touch, without you having to reach out individually to dozens or hundreds of prospects each day or each week.

One solution: Follow up (consistently) with a content-rich email newsletter (some call it an ezine, for e-magazine, others call them email blasts) that prospects actually want to receive and look forward to reading. The key to this is that your follow-up sequences provide content they can use and resources they need.

Providing amazing content weekly or monthly (weekly is best) will help nurture the Know-Like-Trust factor that is required for someone to go from a cold lead to a warm prospect, to a ready-to-buy candidate. The content illustrates for them that working with your company is very valuable.

Here's a formula for a weekly ezine or email newsletter that works really well:

A personal note from you + high value content they can use + testimonials or other social proof + a call to action = potential new clients raising their hand to inquire more about working with you

And this can be done automatically, meaning, you create the content (a useful article, a quick video), and publish it to your email subscriber list on a weekly basis. This allows hundreds or thousands of your leads to receive and consume it, without much work on your end. Eventually, a percentage of them who are impressed with your content and curious about how (maybe even convinced that) working with you will help their situation will raise their hand to ask to speak to you.

Whereby following up on dozens, hundreds or even thousands of prospects a week would be impossible for you to do as a single human being, this follow-up system does all the work for you. And the higher the number of qualified people are on your list receiving your useful weekly content, the more of them will reach out to talk about working with you. That's Leverage in marketing.

Use the "pink spoon" as an ethical bribe. So, the idea then is to build an email subscriber list of people who want to hear from you and are eager to opt in for your valuable content. In turn, this allows you to stay in touch with them regularly, and on a consistent basis.

Now, there is one small challenge here and it is that, whereby getting onto someone's "mailing list" used to be something we genuinely looked forward to (or was it ever?), with the volume of emails people receive today, few people are excited to sign up for a mailing list anymore, rarely doing so.

In fact, they're more likely to want to *unsubscribe* to the countless promotional emails they currently receive than to add more emails to their already full inboxes. Short of adding them to your email list without permission, which is not only illegal but will backfire on you, how *do* you "get them on the list"?

The answer lies in leading with a valuable gift they can use.

Instead of the only way for you to invite them to consume your marketing on a weekly basis with a button on your website that says, "Join my mailing list," shift your mindset to provide a valuable free gift. This "free ethical bribe" should provide so much good content they can use, that it becomes an Irresistible Free Offer (IFO as we call it), one for which they will happily agree to give you their contact information in exchange for access and then begin receiving your weekly content.

What kind of irresistible free content do you give them to get them on the list?

Ideally it's something that doesn't cost you much but will 1) get them to opt in for the email newsletter and 2) give them a valuable nugget as a sample taste of the solution you provide your paying clients or customers. The idea is to wow them but also leave them wanting just a bit more, as does the famous sample of ice cream you taste on a little pink spoon at the ubiquitous Baskin-Robbins ice cream shops in the United States.

What is the ideal format of your IFO? It can vary greatly.

When I first understood this concept and created my first list-building free offer, I simply put together a list of "151 ways to attract all the clients you need." Available on the homepage of my starter business coaching website, this two-page downloadable PDF with 151 bullet points took me two hours to create and helped me build my email list to thousands of people in very little time.

People loved the checklist, and they tell me that it's something they still use today, even when they're working with me.

Later, I hired a former radio announcer to interview me about my (then) ten-step Client Attraction System® and burned the interview onto a CD that I offered for free on my website. This allowed me to ship something in the mail, and therefore receive physical mailing addresses, beyond just the email address. Having mailing information helped me build a database later on for in-the-mail stay-in-touch projects, such as the warm-letter campaign we teach our members or postcard invitations to intro events.

This interview turned into a free CD was titled "How to Attract All the Clients You Need."

There are many other types of IFOs, such as free video series, a special report or white paper, a downloadable audio, telesummit, assessment, book chapter, annual planning guide, even a free book, etc.

I believe in starting small (the sooner you get it published and available, the sooner you build your list).

The ideal IFO should have very good content, something that can solve some of your prospects' or ideal clients' concerns or frustrations, but without giving away all of your secrets. Secondly, it should prompt them to (gladly) give you their contact information in exchange for this free resource. The key is that they understand that in requesting the IFO, they will also receive your weekly tips by email (with an understanding that, of course, they can opt out or unsubscribe at any time, without hassle).

Over time, you can vary it up, as I do, and offer different IFOs. We have free resources available on **www.TheLeveragedBusiness. com** and on different landing pages on the web to keep the engagement going strong.

Understand that building your email subscriber list is an ongoing process, something you'll focus on for years to come. There's never a point at which you say, "Well, my list has grown, I can stop focusing on list building." No, the mindset shift required here is that you continue building your list for the rest of your career.

And once people are on your list, you will continue to provide good content once a week and for years to come. This content will also include client case studies and testimonials, as well as a call to action to reach out and talk to you (or your sales team) about working together. Over time, many of them will say yes.

This one email once a week can be one of the most important and lucrative pieces of leveraged marketing you can use to scale your business.

As a side note, providing really good value in a free gift also triggers the Law of Reciprocity. This concept speaks to an unspoken contract between two people, in that, when someone gives you a gift or does something nice for you, repeatedly and with increasing generosity, you find yourself having a psychological urge to do something nice in return or give them something back.

Studies have shown that the "return act" can be greater or bigger than the initial act(s) of kindness. In this case, in exchange for your IFO and all the goodwill you provide on a weekly basis through your valuable content, many will want to buy your product or work with you, as opposed to someone else. This is simply because you were willing to repeatedly give them something of value.

The IFO and free weekly content is only one of *many* ways to consistently be in touch and move cold prospects to warm and then ready to buy. In simply committing to setting this up in your business, you effectively automate your follow-up activities and leverage your marketing, increasing your results and freeing up your time to focus on big projects.

> ### 5. Your new favorite words are *autopilot* and *evergreen*.

You can absolutely put your marketing on autopilot. Yes, it is possible to clone yourself in marketing and sales by automating the processes that generate high-quality leads while you sleep. Doing so helps you dramatically expand your reach and save you time, which in turn helps you leverage and scale your business.

Right now though, almost everything that is under the umbrella of "marketing" in your company is likely being generated by a person, probably you. While that has been fine *up to now*, it also requires human capital and lots of time, much of which you don't have.

If our original idea is to get you to ten times the impact you're having now or to Seven Figures (by doing ten times the marketing), you would likely not be able to handle ten times the amount of marketing you're doing now. Frankly, no one would, unless you cleared your schedule and stopped working with clients or on anything else in the business.

That being said, it's time to change the current number of hours you spend on marketing, and instead implement systems to automate or replace your previous efforts, producing a state of leverage.

Here's an example of this in action: years ago, I would go on the road each month with several Team members to host a half-day seminar to acquire new clients. I loved doing it, and it was both effective and very rewarding as we signed up very good clients each time we visited a different city.

But truth be told, it was taxing for me and my Team members to take long flights or train rides to two different U.S. cities each month. It was also expensive and took me out of the office for long stretches of time, which prevented me from working on other big projects that would help us reach our important year-long goals.

And frankly, my three kids missed me when I was on the road so frequently, as did my husband, and I came home exhausted from the travel.

Upon moving to Paris with my family, flying to the United States an additional few times a year to market the program was not going to be an option. That said, we had to come up with an alternative to present our program to entrepreneurs who desperately wanted to experience new results.

We decided to *leverage the same content* using technology by recording the same presentation I would deliver from the stage, but this time, as a livestreamed webinar, available online.

Instead of having up to a hundred people in the room, thousands registered to watch the presentation virtually, increasing visibility and no longer requiring me and my Team to travel for days at a time (you can imagine how thankful my family was).

Additionally, this allowed us to broadcast this same content every other day (fifteen times per month) using new webinar technology, rather than only two times per month in person. While this one webinar was being broadcast fifteen times per month in an automated way, I could use my time to work on other leveraged marketing projects.

The mindset shift I am inviting you to make here involves transforming the marketing activities you currently do in person into something that can work for you continuously and without your presence, using technology and the web. This automation is sometimes referred to as *evergreen marketing.*

Evergreen means that the marketing doesn't mention a date, time of year, the weather or any identifiable thing that would place it within a particular moment in time. Because of this, it becomes, well, permanent and continues to be relevant long past its original publication.

This form of leveraged marketing means you create something once and it runs on repeat, every month, every week, even every day or several times per day. It's very exciting once you put it into place.

Here's the mindset shift required to leverage your marketing: when creating *any* marketing effort, aim to evergreen *everything* and then scale it, so that you can use it again and again without any additional effort or content creation on your part. A book does that, for sure, but can take years to write, even with the best of intentions. Automating your marketing activities on the web can be done in a week or even a day, and can then be used for years to come.

So let me ask you this: If you were to look at some of your own marketing efforts, the ones that require a lot of you, and put them through the filter of automation (using technology) and evergreen (creating something once that could be used again and again), what could this look like for you, specifically?

Perhaps, instead of delivering that in-person talk once a month, you can record that talk as a webinar and make it available online. Each time that someone were to sign up for your weekly email newsletter, you could invite them to watch this webinar.

Instead of filling your talk by calling people and personally inviting them to attend, you can begin driving traffic from online advertising (Facebook ads, for example) to an opt-in "landing page" featuring a video of you describing the webinar and inviting them to register online by filling out their information on the boxes provided on the web page.

Once the new attendees register, a sequence of emails (called autoresponders) would automatically send them the webinar log-in information for you, reminding the registrants to show up the day of, and then recapping the offer you made on the webinar, with a link to register for whatever program or product you were offering on the webinar.

Alternatively, you can replace a series of sales calls with a video series, dripped by email to the recipients every few days, again, all online and by email.

The possibilities are endless. And yes, admittedly, this kind of marketing can seem like foreign territory, even overwhelming, to someone who's not used to it, but once you are shown exactly how, it is easy to get the hang of it and this kind of online marketing becomes your "new normal." This is one of the ways our members get to multiple Six Figures and eventually to Seven Figures. It's because they've leveraged their marketing by following a few proven steps.

Not all automation needs to be online, though.

You can also begin sending a direct-mail campaign (although I prefer to call it a warm-letter campaign), sending one personalized letter in the mail to thousands of prospects, every month, without having to do anything but write the initial letter. It's personalized in the sense that each letter is addressed to a particular person by their name ("Dear Susan") by using a database system and mail merge, instead of having the letter be addressed "to whom it may concern."

This is much more personal than the traditional and impersonal direct mail you typically ignore.

This is an example of how technology can successfully be applied to offline marketing activities. Using a twelve-month "editorial calendar" of sorts, a fulfillment house can take your database and do a mail merge so that each envelope and letter is personally addressed to the recipient, "signed by you" with a JPEG of your signature, then printed and shipped to each of the prospects in your database, without fail and without your involvement.

The only thing you have to do is write the original twelve letters (or someone in your office can start them, and then you tweak it with your voice). Then, your autopilot direct-mail campaign is ready to generate untold new clients for you.

The thrilling part of this, once you get your mind around creating leveraged marketing and learning exactly how to do this, is that it removes you from the day-to-day of marketing and can then be scaled ten times over time. And this automated marketing campaign can then run for weeks, months, even years, and reach thousands of people each year, as you add more new prospects to this campaign each day.

This is what we call a marketing or sales "funnel." People enter your marketing at the "wide mouth" of your funnel (with something free, like your IFO) and then over time, using great content, testimonials, and several well-placed calls to action, eventually trickle down to you as a paying client or customer.

Again, this *may* sound like a complicated process *at first* or when you're not familiar with it, but 1) it's easy when you're shown how (much easier than doing all the marketing yourself) and 2) *you don't have to be the one to do it*. It is a learnable, teachable process (we teach this to our program members) and there are lots of virtual professionals you can hire by the hour to implement the setup and management of this streamlined process. They exist and they do this every day.

Over time, and with each new layer of automated marketing you implement, this process allows you to sign on many more new clients and customers each week, or hundreds of customers per week.

These are only a few examples of the dozens of different traditional marketing channels that can be replaced with automated, evergreen marketing. And know that, after the initial strategy, creation and set up, all of these processes can eventually be managed by a junior marketing manager, removing you from any of the daily processes or tracking.

Once you begin to embrace autopilot/evergreen marketing, you'll realize that leveraging your marketing with technology, email marketing sequences and sales funnels will quickly and effectively replace your current manual, time-consuming marketing communications. It also helps you create greater, more predictable results.

Can you imagine the sheer impact to your business that could result from you implementing this sort of automation? It is absolutely limitless. The added benefit is that so much of the time you previously used on time consuming, one-to-one marketing activities or follow-up is gained back. This means that your time can be reinvested to grow your business in other ways, or to simply spend more time outside of the office with those you love.

How would that make a difference in your own life?

What's the impact of applying the Marketing Activator in your business? Lucy explains it to you in her own words:

"I signed up for Fabienne's business programs because I needed more clients. I remember signing up and not even knowing how I would pay for it. Two months later, I had made just over $80,000 by embracing a no-excuses approach. In six months, I wound up having too many clients! Once in the program, we took on a team, developed systems, launched a group program and began road shows. That year, we made just less than $900,000.

"What's really exciting is that I know how much money we will make in the next twelve months already. We will make nearly $2 million. I know that because the program has taught me that making money isn't random. As long as you follow the formula, the money will come in. That's given me more security than any amount of money in the bank." —Lucy Johnson

Leverage Your Accountability

OBJECTIVE:

Predictably reach much bigger numbers every year by having your team be responsible for growing the business for you, and by always knowing where you stand, so you can course-correct in real time.

O F THE BUSINESS owners I've worked with over the years, the majority are initially resistant to setting big stretch goals. At first, this came as a surprise to me. *("Didn't they come to me to learn how to grow their business significantly? If so, why the resistance?")*

I've since narrowed down this resistance to four reasons:

1) *They can't see how "it"* (doubling or tripling their business in one year) could actually happen. They haven't

reverse-engineered how it would happen, which means that it feels too improbable.

2) *They think they would have to work much too hard or longer hours to achieve it.* (They're already overwhelmed, and so the belief that "more clients equals more problems" keeps them on their current plateau.)

3) *They feel alone in getting it done, even with a team.* (The belief that they are the only one responsible for building the business, that it's their role and no one else's, keeps them stuck doing more of the same, instead of going for exponential growth.)

4) *They would feel embarrassed if they didn't reach "it."* (I mean, who wants to commit publicly to a big stretch goal and not make it? This keeps them focused on building their business in incremental steps, rather than big leaps.)

Here's what I know for sure. By virtue of you reading this book, it is probable that you are not interested in having your business stay at status quo. Instead, you are likely interested in or at least curious about moving past your current reach or impact in business, and looking to really stretch and create bigger results.

More of the same, as you know, produces more of the same. If you'd like to achieve new big results in your business, then we must strive higher.

This Activator requires that we put on our big girl or big boy pants when it comes to stretching our goals and, most importantly, *how we show up to achieve them.* The idea is that "getting away with not being responsible" is no longer attractive as much as "being responsible and accountable." It's about having our actions (and our team's actions) be congruent with our stated goals. This requires regular accountability.

For some time, even at the seven-figure level, I too caught myself goofing off a bit, not being congruent with my actions and my big commitments. I was focused on immediate gratification as an act of rebellion *("Nobody tells me what to do. I do what I want.")* I resented not having enough downtime and so I stole it during the day, when I should have been productive.

I wasted time, and stopped hustling to get things done the way that I had in the early days of my business. I simply wasn't taking personal responsibility for my results and this not only set a bad example for some of my Team members, but it also made people on my Team resentful and frustrated. I had wanted the company to grow exponentially, but when the rubber met the road, my actions didn't match. As a result, some of my Team members didn't fully step into being accountable in the business.

Until I did.

I asked myself, *"How would my world be different if I acted with more personal responsibility and accountability? What would actually happen if I tracked everything in the business and committed to reaching my big stretch goals every year?"*

It dawned on me that immediate gratification is incongruent with getting to Seven Figures and beyond. To grow to the next big level, congruence and accountability (yours and your team's) are what will significantly move the needle forward. It requires a new mindset and a new way of showing up.

> **1. Reaching new income goals every year doesn't happen by chance; it's a predictable science.**

You are capable of achieving much bigger goals each year than you currently believe. Growing the business predictably requires getting clear on your goal, stretching a bit more than you usually would, and then strategically approaching this goal with a plan that is reverse-engineered to keep you (and your team) accountable to reaching it. You make it happen by tracking this target on a quarterly, monthly, weekly, even daily basis.

I'm known by the members of our program for what they lovingly refer to as *The Fabienne Stretcher.* When asked what their goal is for the next twelve months, many business owners have either not thought about it or come up with a nice "respectable" idea for an income increase, or an increase in clients. Often it can be to make the same as they did the previous year, or 5 percent to 10 percent over the previous year's revenues.

I will always say to them with a smile, "Sure, if that's what you really want." But I believe that most people creating goals for themselves, their company and their team are really *playing not to lose.* In my experience, it often takes just as much effort to increase 10 percent as it does 40 percent. Sometimes 40 percent is even easier, because it puts a little fire in your belly, the way a "soft goal" doesn't.

Now, I'm not suggesting that you come up with a financial goal for the year out of thin air. It needs to be an educated guess, where you've crunched numbers and, even though it feels like a little bit of a stretch, you do believe that it could be reachable. Without this substantiating, data-driven piece, 1) the goal is harder to reach because there is no rationale for it, 2) there's no real plan for reaching it, 3) because there's no plan, you have no belief, conviction or expectation that you will actually reach it, and therefore, 4) you won't put accountability measures in place to know where you stand at any given time as it relates to your yearly goal.

And when these four elements aren't in place (a rationale, a plan, a belief or expectation, and accountability measures) it can really affect your confidence for the long term should you not reach your numbers. This can really shake you, as it did me, when I pulled a number out of thin air many years ago, and declared it as my goal for a particular project we were working on, only to not meet that goal. I had announced my intention to the team, proudly expected it, and when it didn't happen, I felt embarrassed and, frankly, a bit humiliated.

Here's what happened (and I hope you will not judge me for the elevated numbers that follow. If it makes you more comfortable, bring the number down in your own mind so that it feels easier to grasp.)

I had been hesitant to state a financial goal for a particular event we were hosting, but when pressed, I reluctantly said, *"Well, let's hope for Seven Figures in revenues for this project."*

Was it calculated and were the numbers crunched? *No.*

Was it strategically reverse-engineered? *No.*

Did I really believe we could reach it? Well, I was hoping so, but *hoping* and *conviction* are vastly different. So, *no.*

We did the event, and yes, it was a great event. The attendees loved it, but when the final numbers came in, we fell short and only brought in 75 percent of the stated goal. I felt it was a failure, and I walked away from the experience deeply disappointed. I questioned my manifesting abilities and it produced self-doubt that stayed with me for a long time thereafter.

Instead of reaching the Seven Figures, the event brought in $750K, which is obviously a very lucrative weekend and in line with other events we had done in the past.

Nonetheless, at the time and because I had put my stake in the ground and announced the goal to others, I couldn't see the positive behind the disappointment, just that we were short from the stated goal.

It's the same feeling I had felt ten years before when trying to fill a group with fourteen clients (a goal I created out of thin air) and only signing on nine. The number itself doesn't matter. It's the feeling of falling short that can really mess with one's confidence going forward.

It wasn't until a friend who knows me and my business offered to crunch the numbers with me that the picture changed. He asked me about the number of eligible buyers that had attended the event, what my price point for the program I was offering was going to be, and what my standard closing percentage rate usually was for an offer such as this one. I answered him and in a few seconds, he told me what my revenues should have been based on the data. And wouldn't you know it, it was exactly the number that I had actually sold at the event, not the seven-figure goal I had pulled out of thin air.

This was a huge lesson, one I've never forgotten, and it's changed the way we set goals now.

Instead of using the "out of thin air" approach to goal-setting for the year ahead, or having no goals as some do, there is a more strategic approach. You can look at the following to create a "realistic" goal, but a bit of a stretch:

1) What were your gross business revenues last year?

2) What is your typical percentage increase in revenues year to year?

3) Decide how much you are willing to raise that percentage in the coming year. (For example, if you typically increase your revenues by 10 percent each year, would you be willing to double that for the year ahead, and reach for a 20 percent increase? Would you be willing to shoot for 30 percent?)

4) Where will this increase in revenues come from? More clients or customers? The launch of a new product or program? Increased rates?

5) Reverse engineer how you would make that happen, in a spreadsheet, creating different scenarios of how many clients or customers you would need for each product, program or service, to be able to reach those numbers. (In the Leveraged Business program, we use a Forecasting Spreadsheet template to make this an easier process.)

6) Monitor your progress weekly, as we will discuss shortly.

The point at the end of this exercise is that you create a very specific stretch goal, one that is indeed doable and you feel somewhat confident (even if a bit nervous) that it can be reached with the right plan, tracking measures and accountability structures.

There are many roads to Rome and you should pick ten. Having a clear financial goal for the next twelve months is not enough. Doing more of the same in the everyday of your business will create more of the same results. Big increases come from implementing new projects or maximizing an existing revenue source to full capacity. The key is to focus on what will help you experience exponential growth in the business. It's about thinking strategically.

Start thinking in terms of Exponential Growth Activities, the specific projects you and your team will put in place over the coming year to get you to that stretch revenue goal by the end of the twelve-month period. It could be a new program or initiative, additional offline marketing channels, the addition of online marketing to significantly increase lead generation, implementing a sales team, etc. that will have you take significantly bigger steps toward your goal.

The way to do that is to, once a year, select the ten big-scale projects or processes that will effectively get you toward your big goal, financial or otherwise, even if that plan gets tweaked over time. These are your ten Exponential Growth Activities (we spend a half day creating these at the beginning of each year).

This is simply a process of reverse-engineering your targeted revenue increase and asking yourself, *"If this is our financial/client goal for the coming year, then how specifically will we predictably reach it within the time frame we've given ourselves?"*, or, *"To increase revenues by 40 percent in the coming year, what needs to be in place that is not currently in place? What projects, actions, and new processes need to be implemented?"*

If you have a team, this is an exercise you'll want to do together during one of your end-of-year quarterly offsite meetings. Putting this list together with them (as opposed to you alone working in a vacuum in your office), will create buy-in and excitement from each team member, especially if there's an end-of-year reward for them once you collectively reach it, such as a team vacation or extra paid time off for the whole company.

Each of the ten exponential growth projects (it can be fewer, but we've found that eight to ten gives you diversity) then gets even further reverse-engineered, chunked down, given timeframes and roles, and tasks are assigned to team members in a project management software, such as Asana, Basecamp, etc.

---

2. You love your *ideas*, now love your *numbers*.

What you track grows, pragmatically (and energetically too).
For too many years, I was unknowingly asleep at the wheel of my business, letting others look at the numbers, and not holding myself or others accountable for growth. What invariably happened is, in month ten of a twelve-month year, I would ask how we were coming along with our yearly goal and we would be significantly short.

In that period of a few years I stopped growing the business exponentially as I had when I was tracking everything on a day-to-day basis. I had taken my eye off the ball and wondered why we weren't growing as we had been when I was in charge. What I've come to embrace is that *tracking is everything* and *what you track grows.*

Your role as business owner is to be like a hawk on your progress, not with a greedy, dictatorial energy, but from an *intentional* perspective. What you focus on (and measure consistently) manifests itself. This is true on a pragmatic, practical basis because, if you see a dip in sales, you can immediately increase marketing spend or efforts. Energetically speaking, quantum physics has long proved that what we put our attention to is what materializes. This is scientific.

Predictable growth is a weekly process that embraces course correction. If you don't know where you are *weekly* as it relates to your overall end-of-year goal, and your Ten Exponential Growth Projects, you can't effectively make educated, strategic decisions in *real time* and you will find yourself between a rock and a hard place when there's no time left in the year to reach this goal. Being *informed* about where you stand with your goals allows you to take quick action to course-correct any dip and get back on track.

Once you embrace this, you'll come to realize how incredibly beneficial and productive it is to review your targets and progress on a *weekly basis*, rather than once a month. It's essentially the equivalent of checking in on your business fifty-two times a year, rather than only twelve. It also leaves a lot of time and wiggle room for course correction, if need be, which, let's be honest, is always required, in any business. Nothing ever goes perfectly 100 percent of the time, so it's good to plan for unexpected surprises.

Regular accountability "blips" cause heightened activity and a healthy sense of urgency on a regular basis, rather than having heightened activity twelve times a year, or none at all, as is the case for most business owners who fly by the seat of their pants.

The way to create this type of "regular healthy urgency" is with daily team huddles and weekly accountability meetings with your team focused on the progress of everyone's Exponential Growth Activities so you can get a sense of exactly where you are as a company on your collective roles and projects. When you commit to these *tracking sessions*, and make attendance to these meetings non-negotiable, you will achieve increased movement on your set quarterly goals, and therefore your yearly goals.

Switching to this "accountability mindset" produces dramatically better results and is indicative of a leadership of personal responsibility. But the accountability mindset is not just for you. Instead, you will involve the whole team in being accountable.

---

3. Every team member is responsible for growing your business.

You are not meant to be the only dragon-slayer. Once you personally adopt and leverage an "accountability mindset," you must now understand that you are not the only one in your company who is responsible for the exponential growth of your business. It must become a common goal, embraced and followed by all.

For this to become a reality, the next mindset shift that must occur is the realization that *every member of your team*, beyond their regular "job description approved" day-to-day role, is also directly responsible for getting these Ten Exponential Growth Activities implemented, with the intention of reaching the yearly stretch revenue goal.

Growth is a team effort!

Each role within the company, such as marketing, sales, finance, human resources, technology, customer service, operations (even if *you* are currently wearing those hats until you can hire someone in these roles) has a hand in working beyond their "job description activities." In addition to their regular roles, they too will take on additional projects that will make the company grow.

They too will select their own ten yearly Exponential Growth Activities to move the business forward in their specific area. They will be held accountable for implementing the collective company-wide Ten Exponential Growth Activities.

(If you feel some resistance around this or are questioning whether a team member will actually *want* to take on additional projects to move your company forward, rest assured, we will address how to do this next.)

Your business is an entitlement-free zone. To leverage and scale your business consistently, you must shift your company culture to one where "cushy," "entitled," "fly under the radar," or "not my job" are outdated concepts that no longer exist, at least not in your organization.

This was a significant revelation for one of our members who had a team of practitioners, many part-time, who had been with her for many years, some as many as fifteen to twenty years. They came and went as they pleased, dictated their own hours, clocked-in and clocked-out whenever they liked, and often chose to take vacations during the busiest times of the year for the business. And never, *ever*, did they feel that they had a role in the business other than doing the least they possibly could.

At the same time, the business owner was burning the candle at both ends, working nights and weekends, sometimes not taking a paycheck herself, and watching her business either plateauing in terms of revenues, or, sometimes, making less than the previous years. She was the only one pushing the boulder up the mountain and knew deep down that she was essentially babysitting a group of lazy prima donnas, in her own words. She felt resentful about it, but didn't see how she could possibly make a change.

She couldn't see the light at the end of the tunnel and was too tired to push the boulder up the mountain by herself any longer. Sadly, she admitted that, before joining our program, she had many times considered throwing in the towel and shutting down the business after close to thirty years.

The whole arrangement reeked of entitlement.

Some tears flowed when we shared with her that, no, this is absolutely *not normal* or how businesses are meant to be run, even if it is not entirely unusual. Next, we advised her to make some serious changes, first in her mindset and self-worth around boundaries and getting her own needs met in her business, rather than meeting all her team members' needs, at the expense of her own. Then we gave her some best practices to help her tweak her style of leadership, and finally, in setting the bar much higher in her expectations of her team.

They were either going to stop acting entitled and jump in with sleeves rolled up, or, they would have to go. She was scared to do so at first, but agreed that she really had no choice, unless she wanted to fire them all and start from scratch. The future seemed too bleak to not do anything differently.

In the end, she boldly followed the steps we provided and was surprised that some members of the "entitled bunch" of her team did step up. She was also not surprised that some others left in a huff. Both scenarios helped her turn over a new leaf on the way she was managing her team and in the accountability of each team member. She went on to dramatically increase her business and her quality of life.

Perhaps you are experiencing some entitlement within your own team. Experiencing a change in how to exponentially grow your business requires creating a culture of personal responsibility, one in which *everyone must directly contribute* to the growth of the company if they want to work there, just as *you* contribute to it.

Yes, it requires building a team of people (maybe from scratch) that have a great deal of stamina and enjoy working hard toward a common worthwhile goal. You want to be surrounded by individuals who take great satisfaction in being busy and productive, and who find fulfillment in making a difference in people's lives.

In fact, you *deserve* this high level type of support. These team members exist, at least somewhere in the world. But you must first accept that it is *possible* to have them and then believe that you deserve them.

Otherwise, if you accept mediocrity or entitlement, you are not the true leader of your company, you are in servitude to a group of people who are taking advantage of you on a daily basis, and who know this full well, but who keep doing it anyway. This is not why you started your business, and frankly, if asked whether you would still want to be in this entitlement situation in five or ten years (let alone *one* year) you would probably say no.

So, a shift must happen.

And yes, admittedly, this can be a very frightening shift to make. It can bring up fears that some team members will leave if presented with a new way of working that they won't accept (and the likelihood is that they should probably leave, especially if they're unwilling to see things your way). But your business is not here to provide a cushy existence for people who take advantage of you and your kind heart. No, your business exists to provide a benefit to many, many clients and customers, and you *cannot* increase your impact with a team that is riding on your coat tails, expecting you to do all the heavy lifting.

There will surely be room for this type of person in another company, just not yours. So, perhaps it's time to lovingly release them into the workforce so they can find a better home, one that will fit their expectations.

From now on, everyone on your team is a player and your company culture will focus on collaboration, acting as a cohesive family, with an all-hands-on-deck approach, for the greater good of all. This will be your New Normal.

> ## 4. Your goal is to build a team of intrapreneurs.

It may not be *their* business, but everyone on your team will be running their own "company" within yours. One of the reasons you likely feel so overwhelmed in your business is that everything currently rests on *your* shoulders. Over the years, you've been responsible for sales, marketing, the financial and legal aspects of the business, hiring and firing, training staff, signing on and onboarding new clients and customers, making payroll, handling the operations, delivering the end results to the clients, even ordering new staples and toner for the printer. And that doesn't even include growing the business past its current stage!

No wonder you're overwhelmed and exhausted, working on evenings and weekends, not taking a totally unplugged vacation! *How would you?*

To scale your business further, you'll want to start seeing your business differently. Not *you* at the bottom of the pyramid, shouldering all the responsibility, but rather the one at the top of the pyramid, *leading* a team of people who are each in their different domain, with each *owning* that domain.

Having each team member own their "area of expertise," running it and being personally responsible for it as if it were their own business is what we call *intrapreneurship*.

An intrapreneur *acts* like an entrepreneur *within* an organization. They are usually highly self-motivated or responsible individuals who act proactively, are action-oriented and perfectly comfortable with taking the initiative once they understand what their role is, what their tasks are and how to do them. They like (actually, prefer) autonomy, and at the same time, they like working closely with others in pursuit of a common goal. They know it's not technically their company, but they take responsibility for their "area" as if it were.

Here's an example I'd like to share with you. In a marketing campaign we ran a while back, the team member in a particular position was supposed to set up a pre-recorded webinar to run at a particular time on a Saturday morning. Thousands of business owners had signed up to watch it remotely and tuned in to do so at the appointed time, only to find a blank screen. The person "in charge" had set it up to run on its own but after "pushing the button" had walked away and gone about their Saturday activities with their family and friends.

We heard about this fifteen minutes after the start of the webinar, when lots of messages came in asking what had happened. The problem was eventually fixed, but not without having people who'd signed up for this video presentation wait a full twenty to twenty-five minutes for it. Hundreds of attendees gave up and left, never experiencing the webinar they signed up for, and we lost possibly tens of thousands in potential revenues from the program being offered at the end of the webinar. Obviously, this is never what we would hope for, especially since it was caused by a simple mistake.

Once everything was fixed, I spoke to the team member in question, found out exactly what had happened and then asked the key question that shifted the conversation and forever changed this team member's approach to the business.

"What would you have done differently in setting up this webinar to run if this had been your own marketing campaign, your own business?"

The answer impressed me:

"I would have paid closer attention to the steps that needed to be taken to ensure proper set up. I would have checked in with all team members involved fifteen minutes before Start Time to ensure all items were properly in place before the video presentation was to begin and I would have been online during the event. I would have owned it in a bigger way. I take full responsibility for the presentation not starting on time and I will ensure that this doesn't happen again by taking the necessary steps to plan, set up, and check that all items are properly in place before launch time."

That is what we now call fully "owning it."

That's what you call *intrapreneurship* and it's the true meaning of accountability.

You will love team meetings when you're doing them right. In my early twenties, I worked at three large Manhattan advertising agencies, each time in the media planning and buying department. It involved working on large teams, and, admittedly, I was the low woman on the totem pole within my department.

To navigate working as a team on large client accounts with millions of dollars in magazine and television advertising placements, we would meet regularly, weekly, sometimes even daily. Truth be told, I dreaded these meetings for several reasons:

1) People were often late.

2) Meetings sometimes got moved at the last minute, and took several days to be rescheduled to fit everyone's availability.

3) I wasn't sure I actually needed to be in *all* the meetings (sometimes, it felt like my presence was the equivalent of simply copying me on a company-wide email) and I could have used my time differently and more productively.

4) Certain team members were unnecessarily long-winded and the meetings took much longer than they actually needed to.

5) The pace of the meetings didn't move fast enough.

6) Even after a long meeting with lots of discussion, we sometimes didn't come to any resolution or decision and made another meeting to discuss the same topic again.

Having a huge pile of work already waiting for me at my desk, I felt that this was a big waste of time for all involved, including me. At the meetings, I nervously tapped my pencil on the conference table or my notebook. I know it sounds arrogant, but all I kept thinking was, *"I have so many better things to do! How soon can I leave?"*

Perhaps you too have felt this at one point or another in your own career? Could this be why you may now avoid meetings in your own business for the same reason, wondering if they're actually effective and worth your time?

Fast forward years later and after leaving corporate to start my own business, it was freeing to know that it was just me and that I wouldn't ever have to be accountable to anyone else; I now had the freedom to come and go as I pleased and I definitely did *not* have to meet with anyone ever again!

Until I did.

In my second year in business, I hired my first virtual assistant and we started meeting on the phone weekly to review the progress on certain projects, and plan the week ahead. As my Team grew over the next twenty years to include a combination of full-time employees, part-time help and independent contractors making up many separate teams, I've found myself having meetings again. In fact, several meetings per week.

Because the meetings we now run are based on accountability and are closely related to reaching the weekly goal, which leads to the monthly goal, which is tied into the quarterly goal and practically predicts reaching the annual goal we've set for ourselves, *I actually enjoy them.* They are now based on *accountability.*

This wasn't the case in the beginning though.

After many false starts and lots of improvements and modifications over the years, and a decision to take my own meetings seriously as opposed to continually blowing them off or finding them irrelevant, I turned a new leaf. I have found that meetings can be highly *structured,* incredibly *productive, meaningful* and something you can look *forward to,* contrary to what I had experienced in my early days.

How does one make the switch from not taking their own meetings seriously to treating them like the most important part of the week?

It starts with a mindset shift.

The shift requires that you *think like an owner* (not an employee) and strategically approach meetings as a *system* to get things done, one where everyone's time is respected, important updates are shared, results are tracked, and progress is measured. These types of meetings are where team members are lovingly held accountable to their company-wide stated goals, and issues are quickly resolved because meaningful decisions are made, all on a *weekly basis.* Goals get met because everything is tracked and, if something is off course, the plan is course-corrected.

What I realized early on after making this mindset shift is that these meetings are not only useful but crucial, and very beneficial for all team members. I started showing up on time, if not early. I took them seriously without rushing them as I had done in the beginning. And I noticed that the other members of the team took the meetings seriously too, now that I did.

Imagine what would happen if you had these kinds of meetings with your team every seven days?

Doing so puts you *in control* of your business. It puts you in control of your outcomes. You are never a victim of chance because you always know where you stand in terms of your stated yearly goals, and you're always on top of the quarterly, monthly, weekly and even daily goals you have reverse-engineered.

There is a case for meeting regularly too, as opposed to meeting "every once in a while" or "when we need to." Meeting weekly instead of haphazardly or monthly means that you catch upsets or derailments toward your goal fifty-two times per year, as opposed to only twelve times per year if you were to meet monthly. That provides a lot more accountability and much more room for course correction if needed!

In this new commitment to productivity and adopting a non-negotiable new meeting model, everything comes down to *progress, accountability, transparency,* and *personal responsibility,* on a weekly basis.

Where there is transparency and accountability, there is great forward motion. What you track, grows. Whether you're getting your first team member now or you already have a full team and would like to increase productivity and profit, it's *your* job to set the tone for *"how things are done around here."*

When *you* take the business seriously, have a non-negotiable attitude around how you meet, and treat these meetings as the *most* important part of your week, it changes everything, especially your results and the effort your team puts in.

5. Your aim is to run a transparent, accountability-based business.

Inadequate growth points to a deficit in team accountability.
Without accountability, even team members who are eager to grow
the business let things slide (as you would) because they have so
many other day-to-day activities on their plate. They feel justified
to work on the most pressing things (immediate gratification),
rather than on Exponential Growth Activities, which often provide
delayed gratification.

I have been guilty of having this kind of team in the past AND
of being the one who didn't get her tasks done because no one held
me accountable.

If that's the case, how do you bring your team to embrace
delayed gratification, with an eye on growth? You do so by sharing
the big vision of where you are going as a company and each team
member's individual role in making a difference in people's lives.

Every team member wants to feel significant and that they
belong to something bigger than themselves. It is, I believe, part of
human nature to want to belong. To your team members, it needs
to feel like *the work matters*, and it is your job as the leader of the
company to educate them on the fact that *accountability* is the key
to making that positive impact.

With the right accountability and by tying it to "making a real
difference," team members feel proud to accomplish epic work,
especially when it feels like their own "baby." They appreciate being
a part of something bigger than themselves and when they feel like
their work matters, they actually appreciate tracking how much of a
difference they're making.

**Your company's numbers help you locate the issues in your
business, in real time.** When you have an accountability system in place, visible by all, everything changes. Once results are

141

transparent and everyone is held accountable, you will begin to see a lot more forward motion on the ten projects that will ultimately get your company to that 40 percent or 100 percent growth you set your sights on.

Transparency comes when everything is measured in terms of numbers and each team member is assigned a "number" of their own, tracked weekly. Where many business owners look at their numbers monthly or quarterly, tracking weekly allows you as the chief strategist (as well as your team), to see trends on a much more frequent basis. Instead of identifying a trend over a period of four to six months and not being able to move quickly on reversing the damage, you will see one in three to four weeks and can act accordingly. This makes rapid company-wide decisions and course corrections possible sooner rather than when it's too late.

We teach our members to keep a dashboard or scorecard of everything that happens in the business. Key numbers (some companies call these Key Performance Indicators, or KPIs) are designated so as to tell a story. A team member's number could be the number of clients signed up that week, a financial benchmark to strive for weekly, a number of leads received or a cost per order.

(I recommend starting with just three or four numbers company-wide and to expand over time. Otherwise, it can feel very complex and overwhelming, which is the opposite effect of what you're trying to achieve.)

Eventually, every team member will own "their number" to which they will be responsible on a weekly basis. It is a different number for everyone, and this number becomes for you (and them) like a weekly pulse on whether they (and the company as a whole) will reach your year-end goal.

As a simple example, if you want to have signed up an additional sixty clients in twelve months, an easy way to track that is to sign on five new clients a month. This will dictate how much marketing and how many sales conversations need to be had, based on your typical closing of the sale percentage.

Each team member's weekly number (and results) are visible to all on a master spreadsheet. If their number is down from the stated weekly goal, it is that team member's responsibility to come to the weekly meeting with proposed solutions, rather than the attitude of *"I have no idea why my number is down and frankly, I don't know what to do about it."*

I recommend keeping a rolling thirteen-week average that allows you to see numbers in context, rather than in a vacuum. So, if a team member repeatedly doubles their sales goal, you can determine that she's the rock star of the sales team and reward her accordingly. You can also ask her what she's doing to create such outstanding results and pass on the learning to the other sales team members and create best practices, new processes and methodologies that are then documented in the Operations Manual to be rolled out company-wide going forward.

Conversely, if someone is barely meeting their weekly goals, this is the time to come in to see what could be causing the consistent dip in results, determine a different course of action, ask them what further resources they need, coach them and see what else you can take off their plate to help them achieve their goals.

If you are certain that the goals are fair and the team member continues to produce results below par, despite all the new resources and coaching over a several-week period (at most), this type of regular transparency and accountability will allow you to more quickly replace a team member who is not necessarily a right fit, and solve the problem sooner rather than later.

After repeated coaching and no movement in results, releasing someone from your team who isn't working out is better done after three to four months rather than three to four years.

Your role now is to empower your team to be *proactive* about solving the problem, without you generating solutions for them. This means that you can no longer have a drive-by attitude to delegation. Your role is to coach them in reaching their number each week. You are now here to help them and give them every tool they need.

Team members are responsible for predictably promoting or firing *themselves.* Based on this model, your team continually knows how close they are to reaching their goals (and therefore their bonuses, if you offer this). They are in control of their career and how much they make because they can a) dig a little deeper to achieve it, or b) ask for coaching or resources if they haven't quite met their goals. They drive their results. They are personally responsible and always aware of how they're doing.

Having this information available to everyone creates a positive sense of control for each team member as they are in the driver's seat, with available navigation advice from you if they want it. This can be really exciting for the type of person who takes personal responsibility for their life and career. It creates a camaraderie and group of people who love working together toward a common goal which, in the right culture of collaboration rather than cut-throat competition, translates to a really healthy team of people who like being together.

In the end though, if a person's numbers don't get better with your coaching, or if they're uncoachable, they will realize (often on their own) that it's not working out. It will be no surprise to them that they are probably not suited for the role.

Yes, in life, we must put people first. But in contrast to what might be happening in other companies, you're not here to babysit team members who are content with creating mediocre results. I know that this sounds harsh, but I've noticed over the years that the right team members appreciate knowing where they stand and having this kind of autonomy in their career. They will stay with you longer because they feel in control.

They key to succeeding with this kind of transparency and autonomy is to create a culture that is focused on metrics and key performance indicators, yet in loving and supportive ways.

When a team member knows they are going to be held accountable for certain tasks and benchmarks being accomplished on a regular basis, this also tends to very quickly weed out people who are happy to just clock in and clock out, which leaves you with rock stars rather than people happy to slide by under the radar.

Each team member knows exactly where they stand and has a constant opportunity to take control of their path within your company. Within a transparent, accountability-based company, and with clear opportunities to make more money and advance in the company by moving the company forward, you "put the power" into each team member's hands to either create a very lucrative career path or to be "lovingly released back into the workforce" to find something they're better suited for, as I like to call it.

If a salesperson regularly doesn't meet their weekly number (one that the other salespeople are meeting) you can inquire about what they might be doing differently. If after a fact finding mission, you realize that they're going off script and not using your processes, you can coach them to follow the methodology that works. If within a couple more weeks, you continue to see the results haven't changed and that they're still going off script, you're not really firing them. You can see that the team member in question is *firing themselves* by not following the systems or coaching, and repeatedly not meeting their numbers.

Conversely, the right team members can also see this as a huge opportunity to make extra money throughout the year and continually promote themselves, increase their salary and win goal-tied bonuses, as well as unexpected job-well-done bonuses.

If a team member is not doing well, my view is that there is nothing wrong with the team member in question. It's rather that their role in your company is probably not their life's purpose. That's where we can put any anger or resentment aside and have compassion for them.

By releasing them sooner rather than later, you are doing them (and you) a favor. It allows them to find more fulfilling work elsewhere. Although they might not thank you immediately for it, over time, they will realize that if they'd stayed much longer doing something they don't love, it would have been a disservice for them, as it was for you.

In the end, it's your (the business owner's) responsibility to lead with accountability, so that you are never surprised at the end of the year. Your results have been predictable the whole time.

A keen focus on execution and implementation trumps another brilliant idea, any day. That's how you predictably reach your stretch goals and reach Seven Figures (or more).

What's the impact of applying the Accountability Activator in your business? Sheri explains it to you in her own words:

"My name is Sheri Chaney Jones, president and founder of Measurement Resources Company, where we help government and non-profits measure and communicate their impact and value.

"I had been following Fabienne, a successful business owner who had three little kids and I thought, 'I want to be her.' So I came to one of her live events seven years ago, and even though I didn't sign up right away, I knew that I was supposed to work with her.

"That event was a huge trigger in my life. At the time, I was working full-time in a fairly high level government position with a side consulting business which made about $10,000 per year. I realized that I could not make more than $10,000 if it was just a side business because I also had two small children at that point in time.

"I do not advise you to do this, but I resigned the Monday after I came back from that event. My husband, Matt, was there with me, and we both agreed that I should join.

"The success that Fabienne had while raising children was inspiring to me. I wanted to learn from her because there were other coaches who were teaching similar content, but they didn't have kids. I knew that she would understand what it's like to be a mother and to grow a business without compromising.

"A year after I joined the program, my husband quit his corporate job and joined my business because we had done so well in that one year. We had our fourth child and I've had two babies since I started my business. Now we have four kids and it's been an incredible journey. I have now reached Seven Figures in my business, and I work less than I used to at Six Figures.

"Because I launched my business with Fabienne's teaching, training, and skills, the Leveraged Business process is woven through the fabric of my business. I don't know how to separate our success from everything that I learned here. Accountability, leveraging teams, leveraging my time, how to hire, and even the exercises we do at our team retreat have all come from Fabienne's curriculum.

"I feel so blessed to have found Fabienne at the beginning because I can't separate the wild trajectory I've had from implementing everything that I've learned. It's the accountability from all of the other amazing people in this room that makes me know that I can do it.

"Becoming a member is an extremely wise investment. We invest in our education so we can get a good career, and I'm an academic and a researcher at heart, so to me, it made sense. I didn't know how to market. My biggest fear when I started my business was, 'How will I get clients? How will I market?' I went to the best. If I'm going to learn how to market, I'd better learn from the best. Just like you would go to the best university to get your degree, I went to the best business coach to learn how to grow my business.

"This is the best business investment I've ever made." —Sheri Chaney Jones

Leverage Your Differentiation

OBJECTIVE:

Become "untouchable" in your industry by differentiating your offerings so much that clients stay for years because they get results that (and feel what) they can't elsewhere.

WHY IS IT that some businesses seem to have virtually no competitors? Why do some companies stand out far ahead of others? What's their magic touch? What makes them so unique that they break the mold of their industry and turn everything on its head? That's the point of this Activator, to make you and your business an *industry change agent*.

Let's examine how one business transformed its industry and eliminated virtually all competition and see what we can learn for your own business.

If you have a chance to go to Amazon.com and search for a "girl doll," you may notice that there are many to choose from in the search results. There are the Melissa & Doug brand dolls (around $26), the Alexander Doll (around $40) and the American Girl dolls (for as much as $225).

When initially comparing these dolls online, it may seem that they have many things in common and that very few things differentiate the three dolls. In fact, at first glance, it's difficult to determine what makes them at all different. But then, we look at the price point for each doll and wonder how one of them, the American Girl doll, can cost ten times more than the others.

Upon looking beyond first appearances into the American Girl doll phenomenon, and it is indeed a phenomenon among a subset of young girls, we realize that there is actually a world of difference between this eighteen-inch doll and all the others available for purchase. Beyond the actual product (the commodity or the tangible doll) lies an *experience*, a *lifestyle*, a *sense of belonging* for every girl that purchases it.

What isn't clear at first sight if you're not familiar with American Girl is that there are extras that come with the doll that go way beyond even the book that accompanies the purchase. The customer has the option to purchase a customized doll that looks like her, with options including skin color, hair texture, hair length, eye color, and eye shape.

There are also a variety of clothing options to buy for the doll (a whole wardrobe can be purchased separately, with many different outfits, one for every occasion). Additionally, one has the ability to purchase outfits for the young customer that will match what her doll is wearing. Then, there is a choice of innumerable options for accessories, such as a pet and all the required accessories for said pet, a travel suitcase, ticket, passport, sports equipment, a wheelchair and crutches, a bunk bed for twin dolls, a salon chair and hair tools, strollers, school desks, a camping set with a doll sized tent, an armoire for the wardrobe, etc., all for the doll in question.

That's just what can be purchased. But there are many other differentiators that make the American Girl doll "untouchable" by its competitors.

There are American Girl stores in major cities that will rival your grandest department store, a restaurant within the store where you can not only dine with your girlfriends and their dolls, but also celebrate your birthday with everyone attending expected to bring along their own American Girl doll to the party; a "hospital" for fixing your doll; a beauty salon to have a hairstyle added or an ear piercing for your doll; online games, a line of books for girls on everything from how to deal with bullying, puberty or becoming better at math.

In short, there are few aspects of an eight- to eleven-year-old girl's life that American Girl hasn't thought of, including the building of a girl's character.

The American Girl website explains, "We believe in creating girls of strong character. Facing fears, running into roadblocks, and learning from mistakes? That's life. Responding with optimism and resilience? That's character—the kind we build in girls everywhere, every day through stories and experiences both timely and timeless."

A store on Fifth Avenue in Manhattan, a restaurant, a salon, a "hospital," an extensive clothing line for both the doll and her "big sister." No, this is no longer a child's toy. American Girl has succeeded in becoming a way of life, to permeate every aspect of a child's existence if she lets it. There is a mission, a movement, an identity woven into every aspect, every customer experience.

Owning an American Girl doll is decidedly a *lifestyle*.

Now admittedly, it is easy to judge the unapologetic consumerism that is the American Girl "way of life." I have heard from many parents and relatives that it is indeed difficult to step into the store without the thought of spending way more than originally intended (especially with the prompting of a ten year old).

That being said, does American Girl as a company have any *real* competitors? No, not really.

American Girl has turned an industry on its head. What could you learn from this particular company about becoming a change agent in your own industry? Could modeling this way of doing business help differentiate yours and transform it into one that has virtually no competitors and keeps its clients for years to come?

Let's find out.

---

1. The non-essentials are more critical than ever before.

"I've learned that people will forget what you said, people will forget what you did, but people will never forget how you made them feel."
—Maya Angelou

Your clients' experience makes your company untouchable (not necessarily you). When you first started your business, you likely focused on getting that first new client or customer, delivering the service or product as stated and you hoped that they were happy with the results or product. Maybe you even hoped that they'd send a referral your way at some point or buy again down the line. But it usually stops there.

After some time, many business owners focus on how to make their product or service a bit better, based on client feedback and the hope that clients will stay longer. They focus primarily on making the tangible product or service, well, *better*.

What many don't think about is about crafting a customer or client experience that becomes *a way of life*. You see, at this stage of your business, now that many of the foundational pieces are in place, it is not solely what you *produce* that matters as much as *how you make someone feel* when they are experiencing your goods and services.

It comes down to an *experience* or a *feeling* that they cannot get anywhere else.

Businesses that stage experiences or involve emotion (as American Girl does) are not only able to increase the price of their offerings, but also the lifetime value of that client. The reason for this is that clients value experiences with "feelings" more highly and when they do, they want more of them.

That being said, if we would like to turn your business into one that is a differentiated, industry-transforming business (or at least one that keeps its clients for many years) we must look at the non-core areas of your business. (In the case of American Girl, the doll itself would be considered the core area of the business, but that's not the thing that makes the experience. It's the intangible *character building* and the feeling of *belonging* that makes owning this particular doll an experience unlike any other.)

Even though it may seem counterintuitive, these intangible aspects of your business are what impress your clients the most and make them stay longer.

Here's another example of an industry change-agent.

Paddy Lund, a dentist in Australia with a referral-only, cash-only, no-advertising, no-sign-on-the-door dental practice has a vastly different take on business growth. He believes that goods and services (the tangible aspect of a business) are no longer enough to have a full practice and keep clients for years.

Instead of focusing on the technical, "core" parts of your business, the dental procedures themselves, Paddy Lund's philosophy steers you instead to focusing on the "critical non-essentials," those things on which your customers judge you that aren't evident.

Instead of putting a focus on updating the x-ray machines every year, Lund's dental practice is known for serving tea in Royal Doulton china, and going through a whole tea ceremony for each guest.

There are sugar-free "dental buns" and a state-of-the-art espresso machine. The waiting room is called the "relaxation room." The business cards are "referral cards."

The staff is treated like family and their primary focus is to make *you* feel like family when you visit the practice, so that you feel happy. Happy going to the dentist? Yes! Going to the dentist is now a pleasant experience patients actually look forward to. All team members go to great lengths to make this a reality. And that's why Dr. Lund never needs to advertise and why patients who enter the practice never want to leave.

By focusing on creating an unforgettable experience, this dental practice became untouchable. It has transformed the way dentistry is done and, essentially, it has no true competitors, at least not in the immediate area. A client is usually a client for life and refers many others. And it's never for the dentistry itself.

It is, as Paddy would say, a happiness-centered business and the clients come back again and again for a feeling of warmth and caring, and even a "show," looking forward to the elaborate tea experience.

Notice that these *critical non-essentials* are what they come back for, not for the cleaning or cavity-filling itself. It's the attention-to-detail touches, done repeatedly and with painstaking care, that make the ordinary run-of-the-mill aspects of this business something extraordinary and inspire many clients to refer friends and family.

When companies begin to leverage a few of these "little things" into key experiences for their clients and customers, they experience a state of differentiation (and find loyalty) they've never achieved previously. And when fewer clients leave and, instead, stay for years, while many more referrals begin to flow in, these businesses experience unprecedented growth.

A "little thing" may be a hug that each team member gives your clients, or the fresh flowers and dark chocolate that are always available. It may be the sign-on gift, the picture you send in the mail after each time they visit you, the brownies or birthday gift they receive from you each year. It may be the healthy food, the shoreline views, the feeling of "home" that you provide.

These may initially not seem as important as the way you do the technical part of your work, the thing they actually signed up for. They are likely the things that everyone else in your industry thinks are too small (or costly) to be important, but they are actually the very details that clients and customers really remember and stay for.

Clients initially come for the *technical* part of your business, but they will stay for the *feeling*.

You can absolutely be high-touch in a high-tech world. Right now, your clients feel good because YOU make them feel good, by your presence, your energy, your gestures, the way you get them results in a personalized way, and the way you talk to them. But if we want to increase the number of customers you work with now by a factor of two, five, or ten (to get to Seven Figures), things will need to be systematized, as you wouldn't be able to personalize the experience for so many people.

Now, admittedly, for many business owners who have been personally responsible for making each client feel special, there can be resistance around using *systems* for making people feel special. t seems like an impersonal approach to them. The good news is, your systems can actually feel *warm*, rather than *mechanical*.

As we move your business model to one that is more lever- aged, perhaps eventually (but not necessarily) taking you out of the picture over time, we don't want to lose that connection they feel to you now, especially if it's part of your culture or your brand's essence. The key for continuing that deep connection clients and customers feel with you now is to create systems and procedures that make people feel super special, without you being the one to generate them yourself.

For example, we have been known to send a special "welcome to the program!" treat in the mail to all new program members. It is tied to our message and our tribal language. Hundreds and hundreds of these baked goods have been sent out each year, but I (obviously) was not baking them myself. Nor was a team member of mine spending days in the kitchen baking. No, the orders were generated automatically by our in-house customer relationship management system, and then sent by a fulfillment house specialized in these gifts.

Even though it's a *system*, the effect is still very much *high-touch*. Many who receive these love-filled packages send in a picture of their gift box with a thank you note exclaiming just how very touched and special they felt as a result, and how tasty the treat was.

It's both *high-tech* and *high-touch*. It's different than what others in our industry are doing. And it's something you too can be doing.

This process (among others) can be automated so that each and every client has what we call a Yummy Client Experience, even if you aren't there in person to deliver this experience or high-touch gesture.

Your business is an experience, a theater of sorts. To move from a simple transaction to providing a feeling of "wow" for your clients and customers, look at how your business can create an unexpected experience they'll love. Let the goal be that, each time a client interacts with your business, their senses are engaged or they feel either loved or entertained. Go beyond traditional (boring) transactions and begin to deliver choreographed (meaning, planned ahead of time) experiences focused on *moving the clients' emotions*.

The objective is that the people will remember that moment and want to experience more of them. When your business feels personal, entertaining, memorable or deeply enjoyable, when it can produce a feeling that your clients can't or don't experience anywhere else, they will stay longer and come back often.

Here's an example worth noting: When was the last time you cried in an expensive restaurant and your kids asked (begged) you to take them back soon?

Enter Bel Canto restaurant in Paris. The food is pretty good (at €85 minimum per person, not including beverages) but it is not the reason why people come or why the two seatings per evening are full virtually every night, in every season of the year.

Dining at Bel Canto is an experience that mixes opera and haute cuisine.

A review on Tripadvisor reads, "A quartet of lyric singers accompanied by a piano supports the ballet of waiters. Every fifteen minutes or so, one, two or four of them will perform parts of renowned tunes from Carmen, Don Giovanni, Tosca, The Magic Flute, or La Bohème. The surprise, the joy, and the proximity with the singers create a real emotion. The food is always good but the wait staff make the experience so much better than any other!! I have been back a few times and will definitely be coming back many times more!!"

The only costumes the Bel Canto artists wear are their waiters' uniforms. All the wait staff are new opera professionals and students in the music academy. Their role, other than serving you your meal, is to bring the show to the dining room.

It feels as though you are having dinner on stage. The serving of the dishes is orchestrated around the opera singing, and every aspect of each service seems to be intended to stir emotion and create unique sensations.

As a family, we enjoyed the opera and then were invited to sing along too as eventually, all diners joined in to sing opera together. Everyone in the restaurant sipped a toast together (juice for the kids, prosecco for the adults) as if we were longtime friends and family.

I must admit that my eyes welled up in tears at this feeling of connection. It was such a feeling of home, of belonging, of something bigger than just a night out in a restaurant. This shared moment with strangers who temporarily became family doesn't happen every day.

My children loved it. And while there are many restaurants in the world that I may never remember or wish to visit ever again, my husband and I agreed to come back to experience this one again.

Notice that I didn't talk about the food itself, what we would normally call the commodity or transaction. I am referring to the *non-essentials*, the *theater* aspect of the experience.

When applied to your business, a focus on creating a *sensorial experience* and generating emotions has the capability to turn the usual into something far beyond a one-time transaction and into more of something memorable, a tradition for someone's family, a monopoly they gladly gift you without you having to ask.

The intention is that of "business as entertainment" or as a way to generate a feeling that people can't find elsewhere. Doing so gives those you serve an opportunity to get away from it all, to experience an aesthetic appeal that stays with them. This is about focusing on leveraging your differentiation in the marketplace.

To leverage your business even further, elevate your clients' experience way above and beyond what they would normally expect from others (think *ridiculously different*). Is what you offer currently "transactional"? How could you expand it to turn it into more of a wow experience they will rave about?

---

2. Avoid the "commodity trap" by differentiating your positioning in the marketplace.

"As an entrepreneur, you're in a unique position to create value that makes you indispensable to your clients. By integrating your passions, experience, wisdom, and capabilities into creating situations and processes that help others, you'll find yourself with a much bigger future than your competitors—financially, creatively, and personally."
—Dan Sullivan

Make yourself so unique that you become indispensable to your clients. What is the missing piece between *"Thanks a lot for everything, I got what I needed. I'm off now"* and, *"I'm here for life because this is my home"?*

I believe that clients come to us first because they have a problem we can solve. They want a result and will pay for that result when they believe the value is there. But beyond that, I also believe that clients and customers stay for years when you provide this result *while also making them feel what they can't feel anywhere else.*

Here's what I've witnessed in working with thousands of people each year for close to twenty years:

- Everyone on the planet wants to feel *loved.*
- Everyone on the planet wants to feel *significant.*
- Everyone on the planet wants to feel *heard.*
- Everyone on the planet wants to feel *understood.*
- Everyone on the planet wants to feel *like they matter to someone.*
- Everyone on the planet wants to feel *like they're a part of something bigger than themselves.*

That said, not everyone feels loved enough, even at home, even by their spouse or their children. Few people ever really feel like they are appreciated by others, or that they matter.

I also believe that people go where they are loved.

People go back again and again to the places where they feel significant and appreciated, where they feel *special.*

When your business fills a human need for love and connection, for significance, and for consistency or reliability, beyond what a client originally wanted out of the transaction you present in your business, something magical happens. When you make people feel what they don't feel, even at home or elsewhere in their life, they will automatically be drawn to you and will want to stay, without being able to logically explain why.

This is where I invite you to be unique in your industry about filling the unexpressed needs of your clients and customers. Think of significance, love, and connection. You can't go wrong here. This makes your business indispensable to some.

What clients want is not necessarily the only thing they need. Yes, a client usually knows exactly what kind of results they *want*. They're painfully aware of what's missing in their life. But often, they are also completely unaware of what they *need*. And the two aren't usually the same.

I'll give you an example. If a business owner says they want more clients, or they want to get to 10K a month consistently, they may realize that they need marketing help. We'll call this "what they want."

But underneath the surface, this same business owner may have felt like the black sheep in their family for their entire life. Perhaps they have never fit in, always feeling they didn't belong, like something was wrong with them. Maybe they were bullied as a child and have always felt a bit different than the rest of society—"too much this" or "not enough that."

That feeling of isolation and inadequacy has been with them all their life, even though they can't quite verbalize it. They aren't aware that growing their business without unconditional support is keeping them stuck at their current level of business. They don't realize that they need a tribe of other advancing entrepreneurs who won't judge them and who will accept them as is.

They know they *want* new results, but they don't realize that they *need* unconditional love and support. (This is one of the ways the Leveraged Business program is differentiated in the "business coaching or training" marketplace, among other ways.)

Their "want" is marketing or training on business growth.

Their "need" is a community of like-minded people, a tribe of other black sheep that will make them feel at home for the first time in their life.

Do you see the difference? They are conscious of what they *want*, but not of what they unconsciously *need*. So, differentiating yourself in the marketplace requires that you discern what your clients *want* (the conscious result they seek and will pay for) and what they *need* (the unconscious feeling of belonging and unconditional love that they can't seem to get elsewhere, for example).

And then, *provide both.*

And thereafter, *market both.* Lead with that differentiator.

Going beyond just providing what clients want (solutions) but also giving them what they need (a sense of community and belonging) immediately differentiates you from anyone else in your industry. Clients become raving fans. They feel a sense of identity when they're with you. They begin telling others about you. They happily make the decision to work with you year after year and make it a non-negotiable.

When you continually give them what they want as well as what they need, this prompts your clients to grant you an unsolicited monopoly. And when what you offer cannot be found anywhere else, you become *untouchable*, in a good way, by your industry colleagues. Your competitors will scratch their heads, wondering what you're putting in the water that makes clients choose you over them every time.

(By the way, this is true for your team members as well. Beyond providing your staff a job to do and a good paycheck, the right people will stay with you for years and devote themselves to your mission when they feel like they're a part of a family where they are loved and truly appreciated while they get to do good work in the world.)

> ## 3. Providing unprecedented value, beyond what your competitors are providing their clients, makes the competition irrelevant.

*"Because she competes with no one,
no one can compete with her."*
—Lao Tzu

Information is not implementation, and distraction is the enemy. Another reason that clients will stay longer with (and spread the word about) you over someone else in your field is that they feel they are getting better results with you than with anything else they've tried. That makes it a good value for the money. Providing good value, even unprecedented value, is an industry differentiator. It makes the competition pale in comparison to what you offer.

(Just a note to clarify that I don't see anyone in my industry as a "competitor," per se, but rather a colleague, and yet for the purposes of this book, as the word "competition" is a common word, I'm using it here.)

How can you compete in a crowd of people or companies that provide similar offerings to yours?

You differentiate yourself by *how many results your clients actually experience in working with you.* And a big part of that is getting your clients to actually use your service or product, *as it was intended* and to the fullest of their capacity. Left to their own devices, many clients won't actually apply your solutions to the fullest extent, which means that they won't get the results they had hoped for or that they're capable of.

You can have the best proprietary system or methodology the world has to offer, but if your clients or customers don't get results, they won't stay, they won't buy more, they won't write raving fan reviews or refer their friends and family in droves.

In a world where there are innumerable communications and media competing for your client's attention span each minute, there is a ton of distraction.

The thing is, a distracted client doesn't get results. So, naturally, the way to help your customers get better results (and differentiate yourself as the "best" in your industry) is to get them to *engage* and *consume* your offerings as they were intended.

Here's how I see the formula going:

Help clients *engage* and *consume* => they get better results => they realize that your offerings work better than anyone else's in your marketplace => you are immediately differentiated from anyone else in your industry => any competition becomes irrelevant.

Before you assume that I use the word "consume" to mean "buy more," that's not what I mean to say. Increasing client *consumption* in this case means that, as a strategy, we want a lot of the focus in your business to switch to making sure your clients are actually *using your resources.*

The more they use your resources as intended, the bigger the results they will get, and the more valuable your service will be to your clients. This is about value creation and the more value you provide, the higher in demand you will be.

In more than 20 years of mentoring thousands of women business owners, I have personally found that "getting clients to actually *do* the work" involves three separate elements, each important in their own right:

Content + Context + Culture

I'll explain each element so you can understand it better.

First, the Content:

Content is the "what." This is the methodology, the framework, the step-by-step formula that creates results. It is the "meat" of what you offer, the how-to or the product. When used fully by your client, it provides consistent and predictable results. It is the proprietary system we spoke about earlier, for example, the Client Attraction System˚.

To create Content or a methodology that produces predictable results, it is important that we reverse-engineer how clients will get said results. In the case of the Leveraged Business program, I asked myself how *specifically* I had gotten to Seven Figures in my own business while keeping my freedom (no longer working evenings and weekends, taking two months off a year, many vacations, etc.)

It became clear that there was indeed a *process*, which was eventually turned into a *methodology*:

1. I had leveraged my team.
2. I had leveraged my systems.
3. I had leveraged my time.
4. I had leveraged my business model.
5. I had leveraged my marketing.
6. I had leveraged my accountability.
7. I had leveraged my differentiation.
8. I had leveraged my lifestyle.

There were Eight Activators to getting to a million. It was a step-by-step methodology. I knew in my heart that, when applied fully, this process would predictably get any business to a million in revenues without the business owner losing their freedom or their sanity.

So, reverse engineering how to provide a very specific end result is key to the Content piece. Nothing enters any process or methodology unless it helps you get to that specific end result. And that's what we'll refer to as the Content going forward.

Now, onto the Context.

Context refers to how your Content or methodology is *delivered* and *organized*. It points to how user-friendly your offerings are and whether or not everything is structured so that your audience is compelled to engage with it and implement it. It is about the *environment* in which it lives.

How we've implemented the concept of Context over time is by realizing how specifically our ideal clients (women and heart-centered men) are wired to show up in their business. Here's what I mean:

Solo entrepreneurs are typically high idea-generators, but not always motivated to take things to completion. They love to start new things, but get distracted easily by other bright shiny objects (or other matters at home). *They often need structure and lots of accountability* to engage or get things done.

They are also (especially women and heart-centered men) circular thinkers, rather than always linear in how they look at life. *They need regular check-ins, real time feedback, and time to talk things out.*

They are often busy with children at home or other priorities, even if they work outside of the home. They don't have time to reinvent the wheel. *They need a trusted source of guidance (what to do, in what order, and how to do it exactly, as well as the ability to follow examples that already work), with large blocks of uninterrupted time in which to implement.*

Additionally, many female solo entrepreneurs are often feeling-type people, craving connection and collaboration. They sometimes lose traction when they spend too much time alone. *They need kinship and regular contact with others also on the path to stay excited about the journey.*

In thinking of these needs, we've crafted an environment that includes the structure, the monthly board of directors calls, the large blocks of time to implement as a group, the weekly check-ins, the daily accountability, the loving community, etc.

Let me explain some more, this time, by example.

Many years ago, I ran masterminds for groups of fourteen business owners. I would teach them how to grow their businesses over the course of a year. They would get coaching from me, live retreats, Q&A calls and step-by-step instruction, along with a Facebook group to be able to connect with each other in between our time together.

At the end of our initial year together, I would ask everyone to go around the virtual classroom and answer, *"What did you love most about this first year together? What is it that helped you get the results you experienced?"* and the answer was invariably, "the Community!"

My ego would bristle a bit and I couldn't help but think to myself: *"The Community? What about the hours of coaching, the days I took to create the methodology and Content, the teaching from the front of the room, the hotseats, the strategy and Q&A time? Did they somehow forget about all of that?"*

They hadn't forgotten all of that, but invariably, "the Community" was the answer from just about every person. They craved kinship on their entrepreneurial journey, and my need for significance initially felt a bit crushed.

What I didn't realize back then is that, without the Context of "Community" and the accountability that came from within the loving tribe that had been created for them, the lifelong friendships with other like-minded people also on the journey to big things, *there would have been no significant implementation or results,* or at least not the results they had actually received because they had the community.

The friendships, mindset shifts and accountability weren't part of the actual curriculum (Content), but as a whole, they were just as important. These were part of the *experience* and *environment* that fueled their results. This was no longer an accident, but a predictable, repeatable asset to the program. It was the Context to their learning and growing.

Seeing the immense value that these provided in terms of getting results for the members, we formally built them into the program and these Context elements are now very much a non-negotiable part of why the members get such incredible results in the program. In addition to the Content, our Context offerings look like this:

1. *Personalized Map: your customized action plan for each year, tailored to your needs*

2. *Step-by-Step Directions: trainings on exactly what to do, in what order, with examples to follow*

3. *Daily Accountability: finally, someone to lovingly and firmly keep you focused and accountable*

4. *Implementation Time: facilitated blocks of uninterrupted time each month to implement as a tribe*

5. *Monthly Masterminding: your personal "board-of-directors" to help you brainstorm and prioritize*

6. *Just-in-Time Support: Weekly live support for your burning questions, troubleshooting and clarity*

7. *Supportive Community: the friendship and unconditional love you've been looking for your whole life*

8. *Retreats: electrifying sessions for deep learning, mindset shifts, best practices and transformation*

The important thing to realize about these is that they are not what people join for initially. Members are actually sometimes surprised to see how well these Context elements work to get them results. But they are a large part of what creates the outcomes, as well as the reason why they now stay.

Does anyone else offer these? Perhaps, although I haven't seen it, and not the way we boldly do. And this is what differentiates us in our business coaching marketplace.

And finally, the third element is Culture.

Culture refers to the "experience" that the clients, well, experience when working with you. It's the sense of belonging that only a strong Community can provide, the love and friendship, the deep sharing about personal and professional things, a focus on positivity and mental strength, and the tribal language, among many other tangible things.

It's the combination of all the things intended to make clients *feel something* (such as *belonging* or a sense of *home*) that makes up the Culture aspect, which then makes them want to implement what you say, or use your product.

How does melding all three of these elements (Content, Context and Culture) actually make a difference? Allow me to illustrate it further for purposes of clarity using the program as our example.

Everyday solo entrepreneurs who perhaps had never thought they would reach a million a year in revenues, reach these results (usually within three to five years, sometimes less) because we have created a very specific formula using the three elements we're talking about, using Content, Context and Culture.

Here's how Jen Hickle actually demonstrated the combination of the three C's and how each had a role in helping her get to Seven Figures in just two years [the brackets are my additions]:

"Before joining the Leveraged Business program, I had a good business. It was pretty solid, I had just convinced my husband to quit his job. We were bringing home about $100,000 a year, and our business was bringing in $500,000 a year.

"My business was achieving a goal that I wanted, and I knew that I wanted to do more . . . but I had no idea how to do it. [CONTENT] I did not know how to go to the next level. I had done other coaching programs, but the feminine aspect was always missing. [CULTURE] I homeschool, I have four kids, and doing this program was a leap of faith. I told my husband, 'I know I can do this. I can work the program, I know I will.'

"I am so happy to say at the end of the first year, I showed him the business numbers and said 'This is because I invested in this program.' Two years later, we are now netting $300,000 take-home pay and we have a million-dollar company.

"So much of getting to a million-dollar business was about the community believing in me [CULTURE], getting over self doubt and resistance, participating in the masterminds [CONTEXT] and creating time away from my daily routines to think about the business [CONTEXT].

"I love the lessons and strategy [CONTENT], but the people are what I love the most [CULTURE]. I can't live without them! You can't find people like this, in this dense amount, anywhere else. They are warm and encouraging from the first moment they meet you, and they just love you. [CULTURE] I don't know that I loved myself before I met them! They would reflect my gifts to me, and I had to step up to match that.

"My husband is thrilled about the investment now, he keeps thanking me for taking this risk and taking him along for the ride! He got to quit his job, we have a house and life we love, we get to travel—and now he's looking at the numbers and he sees the proof. If I can do it, you can do it." —Jen Hickle

Do you see how Jen (intuitively) broke down the three elements of the program (not communicated openly to the public) and how each element separately helped her get to a million dollars in two years?

The point I'm making is that, if you wish to leverage your differentiation, you must create exceptional results for clients. To do that, I recommend the use of Content (a methodology), combined with Context (the environment in which the Content is delivered so that it prompts implementation), as well as the Culture (the experience or feeling that the customer can't get anywhere else). This trifecta will produce predictable results toward the desired outcome.

I believe that implementing this eventually makes your business untouchable and the competition irrelevant within your niche because your clients really implement, engage with, and consume your work, which means they get results they wouldn't get anywhere else.

Instead of being a "one-trick pony," provide a "lifestyle" journey. In the very early stages of my coaching business, I helped one of my clients start her business from scratch and, within one year, fill her practice. Then, just when I was ready to continue working with her for another year to get to the next level, she announced to me that she was moving on to work with someone else, a colleague of mine.

I was surprised. My ego was hurt. I blushed. I kept thinking to myself, *"Why would she move on when we have done such great work together? There's so much more to work on."* Well, apparently, she hadn't realized that.

In fact, when I asked her why she was moving on instead of continuing to work with me, she told me that he (the colleague in question) was "more advanced" than I was, that I only offered help on ABC. Conversely, according to my client, he didn't just provide client-attraction coaching, but he went beyond ABC and offered teachings on DEF, all the way through to XYZ (such as creating group programs, selling from the stage, generating passive income, etc.).

She essentially told me that she was leaving (albeit happy from our work together) because she saw me as a one-trick pony. Ouch.

I realized that she might have been right, and that I was:

1) not providing enough variety
2) not providing any way to ascend (or continue) working with me
3) not being innovative enough.

In looking back, many of my clients had been sad to leave and they told me so. They got great value from our work, they liked me a lot, they trusted me, we had built a good relationship and working style, but I had set up my work in the early days to be more *transactional*. One and done.

Knowing that they ideally wanted to stay longer, and I wanted to continue working with them longer, I started thinking about how I would remedy that so that I could continue providing value to my clients and stop them from leaving once our initial work was done.

I decided to extend my offerings and transform my work to be more of a journey on which many of them start and want to continue the whole way. With integrity, authenticity, and love, I decided to make it a working relationship they didn't want to leave.

My plan was to keep increasing the value beyond their expectations, anticipating and then meeting their every need on their entrepreneurial journey. This was very well received. In fact, the clients were relieved that I could provide them the next steps (in anticipation of their newfound needs at their new level of business), and grateful not to have to think about finding someone else to work with.

And this is why so many of them stay for five, six, even ten years.

Providing this "lifetime journey" to your clients can be the differentiating factor in your marketplace too, one that very few people offer. And this is what I'd like you to think about for your own business.

I call this establishing an Ascension model for clients. Most of our members begin in a program we offer to those who wish to get to 10K a month consistently. Once they've reached the six-figure-a-year milestone, usually within twenty-four months but sometimes much sooner, they enter the Leveraged Business program (which as you know is about going from Six Figures to Seven Figures and gaining your freedom back).

After twenty-four months of the Leveraged Business program, they ascend to the Masters program (focused on creating a self-managing business that can run entirely without them if they choose). All of this is voluntary, of course. What the members have shared with us repeatedly over the years is that, now that this feels like 'home', they are delighted to stay year after year, not feeling the need to go look elsewhere.

If they do leave after their initial program is over, to look at what else is available elsewhere, it is not unusual for them to come back to us and they stay indefinitely.

The most important thing to focus on is the *process* of setting up a client journey based on their needs. It's about caring enough to transform your offerings from one-time-only to the whole package. It shows you know them, and it shows you care.

How could you move your offerings away from the idea of a simple transaction or "one and done" and, instead, provide a lifestyle journey? How could you offer ascension or variety from the beginning?

If you've ever heard of Cirque du Soleil or attended one of its shows around the world, you know that the shows provide "a striking, dramatic mix of circus arts (without animals) and street performance that features wild, outrageous costumes, magical lighting, and original music," according to the company.

It isn't just one show, though. There are so many to choose from (*Amaluna, Toruk, La Nouba, Alegria*, etc.) with new ones coming out regularly and being performed across the world.

The idea for each show is the same, to invoke the imagination, provoke the senses and evoke the emotions of people who attend the performances around the world. That said, each show is different, providing *variety*. And so, many people (including me) have seen more than one show, in more than one location around the world, whereby I or they perhaps would not have attended the same show more than one time.

Providing variety breeds loyalty.

A few years ago, we created a brand called Boldheart to house many of our different projects and courses. This included being able to move past just offering business coaching, and into programs such as Boldheart Life (becoming unshakably confident and creating a life you love), and Boldheart Woman (the unapologetic pursuit of pleasure and fulfillment).

It also left room for eventually rolling out future projects such as Boldheart Youth, Boldheart Camps, Boldheart Vacations (which clients have asked for), Boldheart Man, Boldheart Relationships, Boldheart Parenting, Boldheart Publishing, Boldheart Giving, etc.

Whether all of these will come to pass is still unknown. But the reason I'm sharing this with you is to stretch your thinking of how your brand could differentiate itself in the marketplace by offering more than what it is currently offering, so that it becomes a *lifestyle*. Like American Girl, this is an example of what's possible when you are committed to a certain vision or intention of providing many solutions for a person's life, so they do not have to unnecessarily go elsewhere to find solutions.

If there isn't a lifestyle component to what you offer, then it could be a journey of variety whereby you keep the same format but keep refreshing your offerings so that they keep coming back, like a restaurant with a new menu fresh from the market every day (no set menu, just daily menus inspired by what's in season, such as Husk restaurant in Charleston, South Carolina offers) or the variety of different programs offered by Cirque du Soleil.

That being said, leveraging your business means that you may want to make it wonderfully impossible for some clients to want to leave, through ascension, variety, and providing a fresh journey to which you continually add.

This is true differentiation.

---

4. Your Fairy Dust is what will differentiate you for the long haul.

*"Be faithful to that which exists nowhere but in yourself- and
thus make yourself indispensable."*
—André Gide

Get clear on your X factor. In the first few years of my client attraction coaching business, I taught my clients the marketing, the whole marketing and nothing but the marketing. It's what they'd hired me for and so that's what I was going to give them.

At one point though, in addition to working on my usual marketing tactics, I began to grow my own business by leaps and bounds by working on my personal growth (strengthening my mindset and wealth consciousness), understanding the Law of Attraction (the magnetic power of thoughts that draws to you what you think about), and increasing my faith. When applied to my business, these principles helped me take more action in spite of fear.

The results were outstanding, but I didn't initially share these new approaches with my clients. I was afraid that 1) they wouldn't think it was "professional" enough for a business coach to talk about spirituality and personal growth and, 2) it wasn't what they were paying me for.

But when they'd congratulate me on the leaps in my business resulting from what they perceived to be solely my marketing work, I felt like a fraud not sharing these new processes with them.

One day, upon hearing about these mixed feelings I was having, a friend challenged me to host a free teleclass about the Law of Attraction techniques and success mindset principles I was using to attract clients and increase my income with great success, without one mention of marketing. I accepted the challenge and called it *"How to manifest all the clients you need."*

I was nervous to host it, but it was a surprising success. My existing clients who attended the teleclass eagerly asked me for additional coaching around the Law of Attraction and success mindset, even though it's not what they would have paid for originally.

Over time, I started weaving in the personal-growth work, and the spiritual development (not explicitly in the modules, but as a bonus to our existing work) and it is this focus on mindset that now allows what we offer to stand out from all the other solutions available for business owners looking to leverage their existing business.

Little did I know in the beginning that adding this mindset aspect to my coaching would eventually become the secret ingredient that has helped thousands of our members go beyond their current internal limitations stopping them from multiplying their impact and income. With our added mindset methodology, they now produce results they had never experienced before.

Lorry Leigh Belhumeur is one person who is changing the world by virtue of having worked on her mindset. Her goal in life is to eliminate suicide worldwide. She runs a non-profit that heals over 15,000 children and 55,000 family members and teachers per year. What she hadn't realized is how much she was being held back in expanding her work by her existing mindset.

She has been a member of the Leveraged Business program for more than five years and shared her story with me on just how much mindset affected her own work.

Because of a proprietary system we created for her, which is scalable and duplicatable, she can scale her process to make a big impact on teen suicide globally. The nonprofit she runs is now making millions more each year—but that isn't what matters most to Lorry. It is the impact she can have by leveraging her differentiation that matters. Her story in her own words is at the end of this chapter.

To add another few million to a non-profit's revenues just by helping a client upgrade her mindset has been a significant sign. Mindset and working on one's confidence have become our X factor. Yes, I'm clear that it's not what makes someone commit to working with us, but for many, it's what differentiates us and is a reason why clients get results.

I'm okay with that.

Mindset is my Fairy Dust. What's yours?

Deliver to them what they paid for, and then gift them what they really need or want, *for free*. Silk Road Palace, a Chinese restaurant in New York City, had apparently figured out the secret to restaurant success, uncontested market space, and making the competition irrelevant.

Imagine a snowy Saturday night on the Upper West Side of Manhattan. Most restaurants on the block have fewer than the usual number of customers they have on a busy night, and the other Chinese restaurants on the block are completely empty.

Silk Road Palace, however, has a long line of people waiting patiently outside, smiling, laughing and eager to be seated, fully aware that they will continue to wait another thirty minutes in the cold. The expectation was that it would be crowded and loud, the service would be brusque and the food would be decent, at best.

Imagine me in my late twenties, happily and eagerly waiting on that same line with my group of also-not-making-enough-money-to-live-extravagantly-in-Manhattan friends. How does this make sense in a city known for some of the best food experiences in the world?

The secret to Silk Road Palace's uncontested success, its Fairy Dust, was:

Free boxed wine.

Cheap white wine.

From a box.

Served ice cold.

In unlimited quantities.

Obsessively replenished without you asking.

Refilled before your carafe was ever empty.

Yes, the wait was ridiculous, and there were many downsides, but customers kept coming back and crowding this hole-in-the-wall restaurant because the owners made up for it by handing you a glass of white wine as soon as you arrived and put your name down (even if you were waiting outside) and kept refilling it until you paid your check and headed out the door.

And the food cost the same as other Chinese restaurants on the block.

Here are some reviews on Yelp.com, to help you get the full picture:

"All you can drink wine. Free. They were serving the house special Franzia and opening the box with elbow strikes. Pure awesomeness. I dare you to try and finish a carafe before the ninja waiters refill it."

"They will not let your carafes of wine sit empty for more than five to fifteen seconds."

"Yes, free flowing wine during dinner & while waiting to be seated. They don't let the carafe ever get empty. Did I mention the Lobster! For a modest $15 you get a huge platter of lobster (probably about two whole lobster per platter)."

"It's not overpriced . . . they don't charge more for their food . . . everything's standard ($10 or so dishes). They also give you free rice (saves a few more dollars) . . . and yes . . . it's boxed wine . . . but you are paying $12 for dinner and drinks . . . what else can you expect?"

"I went to Silk Road expecting to be disappointed. Free wine? It must be too good to be true; there must be some catch, blah blah. It was everything I thought it would be and more!! I went on a Friday, so it was completely packed. We waited for forty-five minutes and were pushed and shoved, but I couldn't complain that much because they give you wine while you wait. The food was surprisingly good too! Well, I'm pretty sure it was good, by the time I ate I was pretty drunk. Most importantly though, they NEVER let those wine carafes get empty!! Someone is constantly refilling them, even if they're still

half full (half empty, however you want to see it). This is a great place if you want to have some cheap food and cheap wine."

"The food here was sub-par, but it was always packed with a line out the door. The decor was drab, but the crowd inside was always jovial."

Silk Road is long gone, but I remember it fondly and learned so much from this restaurant for my own business.

What is the Leverage takeaway here? Why does this anecdote belong in our conversation about taking your business to a million per year?

Because Silk Road Palace knew how to differentiate itself. And it *leveraged its differentiation* to great success.

Instead of competing head-on with your competitors, find out what your customers really want that no one is giving them (and that you haven't given them yet) and then give it to them in a way that's affordable for them, or for free.

They'll continue to come back, tell their friends and grant you that unsolicited monopoly, as my friends and I did with Silk Road Palace. You'll keep clients for a long time and they'll do all the marketing for you.

Even though it's just a little Fairy Dust, it's how some business owners get to a million within three to five years, by understanding what true differentiation means for them, as American Girl does, and then implementing it fully.

What is it that your clients get from you (your Fairy Dust or "free boxed wine") that they love and will come back or stay for, year after year? Lead with that in everything you do. This is when you can safely take yourself to a place of non-competition.

Bringing *all* of who you are to your offerings sets you apart, even if it doesn't "make sense" at first. Being different means to be "unlike in nature, form, or quality," to be distinct and separate from others.

Whereby many companies look sideways to see what others are doing so that they can perhaps model them, differentiation requires you, *by all means possible*, to be separate and unlike anyone else.

Part of that is your company culture, your way of conducting business and how your employees act.

A member told me recently that she has no plans of ever leaving our program because we are unlike any other organization offering business support. While that may or may not be true in reality, she shared that it is my essence or personality that oozes from every aspect of the organization that makes her feel at home here, even when I'm not teaching a particular program.

This is how I see that we differentiate ourselves in the market-place, if it helps you to have an example to work from:

- *We teach marketing with an emphasis on authenticity, integrity and love.*
- *We're logical and systems-focused, but we are also passionate.*
- *We hug our clients, appreciate them and provide a loving environment that encourages them to be who they really are, without fear of judgment.*
- *We sometimes dance.*
- *We enjoy good food and wine together.*
- *There are beautiful bouquets of flowers on the table while we work.*
- *We believe in the power of dark chocolate and always have brownies on hand.*
- *We send members unexpected gifts throughout the year.*
- *We laugh often.*
- *We talk about personal growth and spiritual development.*
- *And the list goes on.*

This is simply the case because, well, this is who I am and what I enjoy in my own life. I love all of the things listed above. I bring the essence of "me" into every aspect of the organization and I invite you to do the same, as it will help differentiate you from others in your marketplace.

For some, this sort of focus on *enjoying life* and *having fun* while diligently working to make our businesses have more meaningful impact in the world is not what they are looking for in a typical business training environment. That's fine. They're probably not "our people." But for the ones who do love having fun and enjoying life while we work together to create epic things in the world, there is a sense that they've arrived home and don't want to leave. In fact, when welcoming new members, some existing members even say, *"Nice to meet you. Welcome home."* (They started it, I didn't.)

Now it's your turn. Let's weave some elements of you into your business to make it different. How do you know what to include? It's actually very simple.

Look in the mirror.

What are the different facets of you? For example, if you are a multifaceted person who is equally inspired by systems, mindset, community, and loving kindness, then weave those into the culture and core offerings of your business.

What makes you unique and wonderful? Are you someone who believes strongly in non-judgment, inclusivity, and being proud of your "black sheep" identity? Then weave those into the culture and core offerings of your business.

What do you like to do? If you love to dance, are spiritual, love fine wine, adore travel, relish in good food, love hugs and laughter, then by all means, weave those into the culture and core offerings of your business.

When you, the business owner and founder, are passionate about and weave in the things that you love, you will do business with gusto and full enjoyment. You will be happy. Your joy will permeate the organization. Your zest for life will inspire others. These passions of yours will become part of your brand and company culture. You will begin to attract team members and clients who passionately enjoy the same things you enjoy, and have the same values you do.

You, and your business, will become irresistible to those who also like the same things.

Yes, weaving these things into your business means more layers of thought and strategy, more time than your competitors are putting into their own clients and customers. And yet this is the kind of unapologetic attention to detail, based on what you're *already* passionate about and what clients and customers like receiving, that permanently differentiates you from others.

No longer are you a commodity.

Your clients willingly choose to make your business their home.

What's the impact of applying the Differentiation Activator in your business? Lorry explains it to you in her own words:

"I help heal children that have had adverse childhood experiences and give them hope for a future that they never imagined would be possible.

"Before I met Fabienne, I'd been looking for a business coach and was introduced to her from a Leveraged Business member. Fabienne was speaking at her Mindset Retreat and when I walked in the room, she was standing there hugging everyone. Before I made eye contact with her, I just knew that I was going to work with her. There was no question.

"At that time, I was successfully running a large non-profit business. I got by on that, but my mindset still had a lot of baggage. I, myself, was a child with a lot of adversity, so I carried that with me. I went to the Mindset Retreat and had an amazing, unbelievable breakthrough. It was a tipping point, really.

"I went back to the office and immediately started putting things into action. I did exactly what Fabienne said from that point on.

"Our revenue was in the low Eight Figures when I came in and, again, it was successful, but there was gunk in the way. My business was stable even during the 2008 recession. We didn't lose income, but

we were just kind of hovering for many, many years. In the last five years, I can document that we've grown exponentially since then. Five years ago, we were serving about 5,000 kids. Now, we're serving over 15,000.

"It's so amazing and I can't stress enough that, for me, it was about feeling deserving. It was feeling like I am enough. It was feeling that I deserved the highest amount of support possible. All of those things that I had never dreamt of before." —Lorry Leigh Belhumeur

Leverage Your
Lifestyle

OBJECTIVE:

Release yourself from the day-to-day of your business with a second-in-command you trust so you can scale to a million for more, while living an ideal life of freedom.

YOU PROBABLY didn't start your business (and then decide to grow it to Seven Figures) to work more hours and have less time off than you would by working for someone else! At the same time, it's totally understandable that you may not have started your business with the specific intention of creating a Lifestyle Business, one that promotes the lifestyle you want to live. For you, that could mean more time with your family or friends and for others, moving across the globe, lots more travel, or living adventurously.

The good news is, how you choose to upgrade your lifestyle through your business is your choice and, whatever that choice is, it's absolutely possible.

As we've been talking about from the beginning of this Leverage Your Business "conversation," I will ask you this again:

Does your business work for YOU or have you become trapped into working FOR your business?

If you aren't quite certain how to answer this, ask yourself this, again and again:

"If I were to disappear from my business for a full twenty-four hours, a week, or even a whole month, with very few (if any) check-ins and without any daily involvement, would my business continue to thrive without me? Would my team be holding on for dear life, not wanting to make a single move or any decision until I returned? Or would doing so possibly bring everything to a standstill, or, worse, create a dramatic setback?"

And then, *"How do I feel about my answer, specifically?"*

Just be honest with yourself. (There's no right or wrong answer. It just is.)

At the same time, let us *future pace* to a few years from now.

If you continue to be honest with yourself, and without judgment, would you be super happy working the way you do in your current situation (number of hours, level of involvement with clients and customers, geographic location, days of the week, involvement level of managing your team) if ten years from now, you were experiencing the exact same lifestyle?

Again, no judgment. This is just an opportunity to think this through and a bit of a reality check.

If you're not yet enthusiastic about the quality of life that your business currently affords you, do not worry. It doesn't have to be this way, and there are many options to increase that quality of life rapidly. This is about using your business to Leverage Your Lifestyle by taking the steps necessary to create a Lifestyle Business, should you want to do so.

Admittedly, the ideas in this Activator can be confronting to some, and may seem unreasonable and even illogical to you, depending on your current mindset. Or, perhaps this is right up your alley and you can't wait to dive in. Either way, there is value here in the idea of creating a Lifestyle Business, whether you would ever consider moving across the globe, or simply spending more time off from your business in the same place you have lived for the last forty years with no intention of ever leaving. The mindset shifts required for either are below.

1. Money alone isn't everything.

"One cannot be free from the stresses of a speed- and size-obsessed culture until you are free from the materialistic addictions, time-famine mindset, and comparative impulses that created it in the first place."
—Tim Ferriss

Spoiler alert: Reaching Seven Figures in your business is anti-climactic. In 2008, I made a decision that I was going to take my business from more than $350,000 in gross revenues and cross the million-dollar threshold within twelve months. I mapped out my plan of how I would do it and then flew in my two virtual assistants to spend two days with me.

We gathered in a bleak hotel conference room near my house and I shared this plan with them. During those two days, we all committed to my big vision, we strategized how we would get there, we put timelines in place, and got to work on the marketing campaigns needed to get the business to Seven Figures. And by October of 2008, just nine months into the year, we had already done it!

We had crossed the million-dollar mark in revenues.

The thing is, I barely noticed it.

I had been so focused on actually getting to the finish line that I barely realized we had crossed it. When it dawned on me that we had, I called my husband (who was still working a corporate job) and said, "You know, I think I might have crossed the million-dollar mark yesterday. Does this mean we should open some champagne tonight?"

And we did, being grateful for this milestone.

But there were no gleeful shrieks of joy, giddy tears running down my face, or any sort of jumping-up-and-down motions. No, it felt like another day in the life of my business, mixed in with a bit of disbelief.

And here's the interesting part. In guiding countless business owners past this previously elusive seven-figure milestone, I noticed the same thing. They were grateful, of course, but it wasn't as if their whole life had changed either.

It was just another (good) day in their business. Kind of like when you ask a twelve-year old on their birthday how it feels being twelve. They usually say, *"It feels the same."*

Whenever I share this with aspiring business owners, they don't always believe me at first. But when I elaborate and share with them that crossing the actual *threshold* that most people think brings you gratitude and joy, is *not* the thing that you're actually grateful for.

No, it's not about the *money* when you cross that million-dollar mark. That's not the part you actually celebrate.

Yes, there is something tremendous about looking back on all the lives you've changed as a result of reaching that big milestone. And yet, it's not about the money as much as the fact that *the money is just a consequence of changing so many lives for the better.* But even that isn't all of it.

What struck me the most was this:

It's about who you had to become as a person in the process of reaching that milestone.

What struck me at that (rather anticlimactic) moment and for countless members who've crossed the million-dollar threshold within our program is *how much we had to grow personally* to become a seven-figure business owner, rather than it being about the money itself.

All the courage that was required, the belief, the faith, the mental strength, the willingness to go through the thick and thin, to persevere, to dig deep, to stay committed. That's what changes you most about reaching new levels (same with the six-figure level, actually.) I presume that this is the case for athletes as well.

This shift in the person you are now, as a result of achieving your audacious goal, is something that no one can ever take away from you. It emboldens you like very few other things can. *That* is the real gift, not the money. (Although it is true that buying yourself some nice things is fun too.)

Because of this new milestone, you begin to believe in yourself and your abilities like never before. And that, my friend, is priceless. It makes you feel like you can do anything going forward.

Time (and how richly you use it) is your most valuable asset, not money. In the end, yes, the money is great! You (hopefully) have more consistent cash flow, you have the ability to hire more people to do things you don't love to do or don't have the bandwidth to do, you give more to charity (or build more schools in Africa, as we have). And yes, you may even get yourself a bigger house and a nicer car, as one typically does in circumstances like these.

What I've learned over the years is that these things are good at first, and they are exciting, but they are not the *real* gift of getting your business to that next really big level.

Gaining more time and more choice in how you use that time is the next big gift.

When you've worked hard to leverage your team, your systems, your time, your marketing, your business model, etc. you realize that you've put a lot of effort (and mostly time) into your business, *time that you cannot get back.*

And there gets to be a point in a business when you've grown it to multiple Six Figures (or Seven Figures), where you really start to think that more money won't bring you as much happiness as would *more time* to truly enjoy your life. This is where your lifestyle comes in.

Getting your business to the seven-figure mark isn't really about the money in the end, no. It's about giving you options, *the ability to choose how you want to spend your time and energy*, who you want to be with.

It is about having a *choice*. That is the real reward. And this is where the creation of a Lifestyle Business comes into play.

2. The tail can very rapidly begin to wag the dog.

"Embrace the idea of having less mass. Right now you're the smallest, the leanest, and the fastest you'll ever be. From here on out, you'll start accumulating mass. And the more massive an object, the more energy is required to change its direction. It's as true in the business world as it is in the physical world. Mass is increased by: long term contracts; excess staff; permanent decisions; meetings; thick process; inventory (physical or mental); hardware, software, and technology lock-ins; long-term road maps; and office politics. Avoid these things whenever you can. That way, you'll be able to change direction easily. The more expensive it is to make a change, the less likely you are to make it. Huge organizations can take years to pivot. They talk instead of act. They meet instead of do. But if you keep your mass low, you can quickly change anything:

*your entire business model, product feature set, and/or mar-
keting message. You can make mistakes and fix them quickly.
You can change your priorities, product mix, or focus. And
most important, you can change your mind."*
—From the book *Rework,*
by Jason Fried and David Hansson

Growth sucks cash. At every significant level of growth in the
trajectory of any business, one has to invest more than previously
expected. For me, it usually had to do with hiring more team
members, and as a result, a larger office space. At other times, it
meant investing in doing more marketing or online advertising,
technology upgrades, equipment, etc. Sometimes, it even had to do
with getting some additional topic-specific coaching, mentorship or
consulting to address a particular issue or get better in a particular
area. The idea though, is that rarely if ever have I moved up significantly in the business without some additional (often significant)
level of investment.

I remember a defining business conversation with my husband
in 2009, less than a year after reaching that first Seven Figures and
after which he quit his corporate job to come on board to help me
run the business as CEO. We had set our sights on eventually doubling the business to two million, but we also knew it would require
a lot more fully-committed help than the (albeit great) part-time
team of virtual assistants we had in place.

At the time, we felt that we needed people who were full-time
employees, 100 percent focused on our business and *only* our
business, individuals who would turn things around quickly for us,
rather than virtual, part-time team members who sometimes were
forced to reluctantly say to us, *"I'll be happy to do that in a couple of
weeks, after I finish two other big client projects."*

We talked at length around the much greater expense
and commitment required to take on full-time employees
and, after weighing the pros and cons (stay where we are vs.

hustle-to-make-it-happen-even-though-it's-expensive because there doesn't seem to be a choice) we committed to doing whatever it would take to replace our entire virtual, part-time team with a handful of full-time employees. Real people, who would require real desks, in a real office, and who had real families.

Wow.

We quickly hired four employees and rented a six-bedroom house a one-minute walk from ours to house all of these new team members (the situation involving putting multiple desks in our living room at home was no longer going to work).

Could we really afford it all at first? Barely. It was definitely a stretch, but we understood that if we hustled to bring in a lot more new clients (which meant more marketing, sweat equity and longer hours than we were used to) while hurrying to bring the brand-new team members up to speed so they could quickly fulfill a role that would have them pay for themselves and more within about three months, that initial investment we would be worth it.

And we did it. But that growth really sucked cash, as did hiring more full-time team members after that and moving into increasingly bigger offices, ones that carried a contract for a five-year lease (!)

All of these fixed monthly expenses and salaries (upward of one hundred thousand dollars a month) meant we went into an over-drive of workload just to keep up the pace, to fulfill the agreements, a pace we had never expected. Yes, the business continued to grow, but the expenses never lessened, and this lasted for years. It quickly began to feel that we were trapped and that our business owned us, rather than us owning it.

Was taking on all these "traditional business growth" expenses the right way to do it? Maybe. I'm still not sure.

If I had the chance to do it all over again with what I know now, would I find a way to achieve the same sort of steady growth without the hefty fixed salaries and business trappings with five-year contracts? *Absolutely.* I know now that I would find a way to do it without all the proverbial handcuffs and all for much less.

Why? Because *it affected my freedom.*

You see, as the business and personal expenses grew, my freedom lessened. I went from having lots of choice as to how I used my time to feeling like I needed to continually "feed the machine," working more than I had in the beginning, just so I could pay the expenses.

And I've since seen that this (often predictably) happens to a lot of people who reach Seven Figures for the first time, where they fall into the trap of needing to feed the machine, rather than being focused on the quality of their life.

But it doesn't have to be this way.

My loving advice as you apply the Leveraged Business Activators that will take your business to Seven Figures and beyond is to *keep things simple* as you experience growth and begin investing in what will take your business to the next big level you seek.

Be very prepared for the fact that growth sucks cash. It's a fact, and a rite of passage. Invest in your business, but choose flexibility whenever possible, rather than getting into permanent situations that end up running you and making you work harder to keep the train moving. Invest in growth, but just do so *strategically, without sacrificing your lifestyle.*

Ask yourself if there are alternatives to the traditional "successful business" trappings.

- *It's not because other people have a large office that you need one. Do you really need an office, or could you build a team that is hybrid, sometimes working from home, and sometimes meeting you at a coworking location?*
- *Do you really need all those full time team members, who require desks and computers and all the traditional things that come with employees? Or could you hire more freelancers*

and independent contractors, who work from home and "own their own stuff"? What about having full time employees but no physical location, meaning, your staff works remotely?

• *Do you really have to drive to your client meetings (and have a car to do so) or could you do things more virtually, including the delivery of your work, using video conferencing?*

Remember, you have it within you to be bold enough to go against the grain and do only what fuels your ideal lifestyle. You deserve it.

Is it necessary, nice, or neither? We've established that it's *very easy* to go overboard with the team, the expensive office, the splashy $50K rebrand, the employee bonuses, and anything else you start paying for that didn't used to be part of the regular expenses within the business. It becomes an even more slippery slope if you've also added considerable new "bling" to the *personal* side of your life, such as the new much bigger house, the new car(s), the beautiful new things you feel you can now afford.

Here's the thing, though. I've discovered that all businesses seem to go through "cycles" like that of nature, as one spiritual teacher once told me. And it's not unusual to buy exciting "toys" or make large business investments in quick succession when you're experiencing the "summer cycle." What eventually seems to happen though, is that many businesses, at one point or another, also experience a "winter cycle."

Nothing is always "rosy" 100 percent of the time. That's life. And as with anything in life, there will be ups, and there will also be dips. The fact is, things sometimes change in the marketplace; sales dip, your marketing isn't always going to work as well as it used to, your online advertising isn't always going to generate the leads as zealously as it once had; team members sometimes leave with their expertise and you have to start all over again; as well as a host of other reasonable events you hadn't expected.

How would you prepare for this if you were to experience a winter cycle in your business?

Make strategic decisions as you grow, so that you can stay nimble and not have the proverbial tail wag the dog, meaning, the business runs you, as opposed to you running it. Keep your eye on having a lifestyle business as you continue to grow, taking a hard and honest look at every aspect of your business and rethinking it.

Take some time to think about all of your business expenses (even personal ones, for that matter). Go through your credit card statements. Question *everything*. Is it necessary, is it nice, or is it neither? If it's necessary, keep it. If it's "nice," make a strategic decision. If it's "neither," then it's running you and you likely don't need it.

In our own business, we now have a "hybrid" model of team: some full time employees in key areas (marketing, finance, operations), supplemented by many virtual, part-time team members, freelancers and independent contractors, but no physical office space to gather in person as we all currently work remotely, from home.

Why no office? We realized that we were acting in "old-school" ways of doing business. We questioned the practice of working in the same physical space or geographic area as the one in which your business is located. Did it really have to be so in this day and age? Could we not forgo this and live across the world from our team?

Well, we didn't know at first. We decided to test the viability of "going virtual" for just one month and announced it to the team. We shared with them a long list of the benefits for them (with no more lengthy commutes, they would have more time with their families and friends, for pursuing hobbies, working out and for self care, etc.) It was so successful that it was actually the team's request that we go virtual as a company going forward.

We have since fully released the idea that a physical office space is required for successfully running our business. And even if we had an office for our employees, we've released the idea that we (my husband and I) would need to be there physically on a daily basis. Using today's technology and co-working spaces, you can (and we do) all work remotely and very successfully.

How does it work? Well, for example, while our program has members around the globe, it is headquartered in the United States. At the same time, my husband and I work and enjoy living in Paris, France with our three children. The way we've made this work is by heavily relying on affordable technology (which I discuss below) and virtual conferencing, which has drastically reduced the need for having an actual office or doing in-person meetings. We've since become very adept at hosting truly engaging three-day live meetings online, using a proprietary methodology for making meetings a highly focused and engaging experience that attendees world wide love.

Doing so has allowed us to attract more English-speaking members from around the globe, whereby it wouldn't have been either possible or convenient before. This is true leverage.

Obviously, your business will be different, but this is an example of how it can be done, so that you increase your quality of life in an affordable way. In the end, the office was nice, but absolutely not necessary.

Perhaps there are things in the current iteration of your business that fall in the same category of "not necessary." Would this be a good time to no longer have this be part of your business?

A caveat: the one thing I will always invest in *significantly*, and without question, is coaching and mentorship. These are priceless to business owners and quite the opposite of a "luxury," falling more into the strategic "necessity."

I have never been without a highly successful business coach (or part of a high-level business mastermind, or both simultaneously) to guide me in growing my own business strategically, and I never will be without one. I have spent as little as $5,000, $25,000 and even as much as $100,000 a year on working with a business coach, and these are some of the best investments I have *ever* made in myself and my business, as the return-on-investment was often tenfold.

Investing in the right coaching pays for itself in spades and I enthusiastically recommend you get coached or join a full support business growth program.

3. Yes, you can (successfully) go virtual.

"I've embraced innovation and current technology to create a decentralized collaborative structure. I have put to rest more traditional work norms such as working hours, geography, headquarters, etc."

—Tim Ferriss

You can run your business totally remotely with the right technology tools and automation. Years ago, I had a wonderful employee, an operations manager who by choice commuted three hours a day (sometimes more, depending on traffic) to our offices in Connecticut each morning to help us run our company. I thought it was a crazy idea at first, but she insisted that she didn't mind the drive and that she was willing to do it. We worked this way for five years and, with few hiccups, it went really well.

After a few years though, we agreed that it would make a lot of sense for her to work from home at least a few days here and there, to cut down on her time-consuming travel and relieve a persistent foot injury her doctor believed was due to the driving. Personally, I would never have been able to drive as many hours a day as she did. That said, I admired her for her willingness, dedication and perseverance in doing so.

We managed to set up some systems for her to work remotely when she could to oversee not only the operations of the business, but also the team. That way, she could manage everything virtually even while we were all physically in the office for a couple of days a week, while the other days, she would travel to be with us in person.

It seemed to work well at first, but a few months later, she began to have significantly more pain in her foot and her doctor advised her to stop the long commutes. I was absolutely fine with it, urging her to set up shop in a spare bedroom for good. I knew in my heart that, with today's technology, we could make it work, and I so admired her work and loved her as a friend that I was willing to do whatever it took to make her happy.

Then, one day, she gave her notice. She came into my office and told me she was unable to work remotely and had taken another job close to her home. She believed at her core that she was unable to manage the team when she couldn't be side-by-side with them. I tried to reason with her, showing her that she could indeed be a great virtual manager and run the operations remotely, that it could be done.

But I don't believe that she was ready to wrap her mind around that. And so, after five years together, we sadly lost one of our most dedicated employees at that time. I wonder what would have been different if we could have imagined this company running smoothly (relatively!) with no one being in one single central location and all of us relying on technology and automation to work rather seamlessly together.

Today, there are many technology tools that can be used for the most important categories of your business. Here are some categories for which we use online tools or software:

FINANCE
- payroll and HR software
- bill payment and accounts payables
- bookkeeping and financial record keeping/reporting
- financial payments and receivables
- time tracking and invoicing for independent contractors
- data metrics and reporting

CUSTOMER SERVICE
- web-based communication service for real-time website visitors
- web-based phone and SMS
- virtual customer service/phone answering system with receptionists
- email-based ticketing system for support cases and troubleshooting
- web-based calendar scheduling system

OTHER
- web-based calendar, email, file sharing and word processor/spreadsheet
- web-based surveys and online forms
- project management tool and task tracking
- team chat communication
- video conferencing and screen sharing for individuals and groups
- web-based team reporting and one-on-one feedback communication
- note tracking and journaling
- web-based conference calling
- web-based screen sharing and recording
- recording presentations
- recording videos and audios on your computer

MARKETING
- text messages via CRM automation software
- CRM, eCommerce, email marketing
- membership site with CRM automation software
- web platform for websites
- video hosting
- live video broadcasting
- live evergreen webinar broadcasting

- email delivery service (various IP addresses to ensure deliverability/not spam)
- Facebook Ads management and reporting
- connection application to link various tools, systems and applications
- web traffic data, reporting and metrics
- online chat tool for webinar/video broadcasts
- text messaging software
- web-based site review tool with editing
- video editing/production
- audio editing/production
- photo editing/production (and free online photo editing)
- captions for videos (Facebook, YouTube)

We've tried many versions for each category, and for now, we've settled on our favorites. Admittedly, you will likely never need all of these and technology changes very quickly, so perhaps by the time you read this, we may have already added new ones and stopped using old ones. These are listed as examples of resources to show you what's out there in terms of resources for running your multiple seven-figure or eight-figure business remotely, from wherever you like, whether it's a treehouse in your backyard, or across the globe, with the focus being a lifestyle you love.

---

4. Relax, you're not the one who should be running your business.

"As it was 3,000 years ago, it is today—some people naturally come up with the big ideas while others can be relied on to make those ideas happen."
—Gino Wickman

Don't trust yourself to run your business, because someone can (likely) do it much better than you can. There is a mistaken belief, a deep seated one, that the one who *starts* an entrepreneurial venture is the one who must run the day-to-day operations of it. A pride thing? A control-enthusiast belief? Yes, probably both of these. Again and again though, when you study those who lean toward entrepreneurship, this doesn't seem to make logical sense.

After years of working with thousands of small-business owners, spanning "from scratch" sole practitioners to million-plus-revenue entrepreneurs, it is clear that (in the vast majority of cases) the person who *creates a business* is simply not wired to successfully run it *once it has reached a certain point*. The Leverage Point, that is. The risk-taker archetype is *not* the one who will enjoy running the processes of a systems-run business. Far from it.

That will require someone who is *intuitively* consistent, who can't help but be excruciatingly reliable (not that the owner isn't, but just in a different predictable way) and focus on crossing all the T's and dotting all the I's, all the time. Someone who loves procedures, procedures, predictability, accountability, checklists and things running on time and on schedule. And the likelihood is, *that's not you.*

Most businesses rely continuously on the business owner for its day-to-day operations. In many cases, clients and customers are used to working with the owner, the vendors have long-term relationships with the owner and the team members don't want to make a move on anything without the owner's approval. That means that the owner (you, in this case) needs to be involved in every single miniscule aspect of the business, and it's what drives many of them to want to run away, or experience burnout, whichever comes first.

But as we've been discussing since the beginning of this Leverage conversation, there gets to be a point in the journey of your business where you must surrender to the fact that, *"What got you here, won't get you there."* To scale your business further, or actually enjoy your life at the seven-figure-plus level, you must eventually remove yourself from the day-to-day operations of your business, even if it seems impossible or unfathomable now.

For you to leverage and scale your business, while gaining your life back, it is now time to shift your mindset to allow *someone else* to step in and do the work you don't enjoy doing: the minutiae, the management, and making sure everything gets done well (and without you).

Yes, these people exist and all they want is to make order out of your business and keep it running smoothly for you.

You deserve a strong string to your helium balloon. Part of having a business that allows you personal freedom as well as the freedom to do only your "uniquely brilliant work" is to create a self-sustaining business, one that runs without you being involved in the day-to-day. And that means that you must now totally replace yourself in the day-to-day operations of your business.

All this time, you've been shouldering all the pressure of your business (mostly) on your own, not only the big ideas, but the grueling, daily details. At this point, you don't have much choice if you want to grow farther. It's now time for you to realize that you deserve hiring someone amazing who will completely take over the daily operations of your business. We're talking about someone who will be your rock and keep you stable, but also who will respect you for your brilliance and give you enough freedom to do your "visionary thing."

I've long thought about the analogy of the helium balloon that, without a string, flies aimlessly and either goes up into the ether, gets stuck in a tree for good or eventually gets deflated and drops to earth. In a way, that helium balloon is likely *you.*

But think about this . . . What would happen if you had a reliable, strong string that allowed you to do your work in this world, in only the way you could do it, but that kept you stable, that guided you, without over-controlling you? That is what a reliable second-in-command can do for your business.

To leverage even further, you will benefit from having this second-in-command (what you might call a general manager if you've got a larger small business or an operations manager or director if you've just a handful of employees). Having this type of person to run the operations of your business for you will be the key to leveraging your lifestyle.

Having this person (someone who is likely wired completely differently than you) to run your business in a reliable way will allow you to trust that things will work smoothly when you're not there and removes you from the day-to-day operations to focus on more important things, whether it's growing your business or enjoying well-deserved (extended) time off.

How do you find a second-in-command? Look for people who like specificity, who like to focus on priorities, reach stated objectives, appreciate strategy and embrace accountability. The best people for this type of high-level support love to have things documented, with instructions for everything. They are detail oriented and work well when they know what the priorities are.

They appreciate having systems and procedures established and followed, to create (mostly) undeviating processes, and therefore, results. They follow plans, design timelines and have others follow them. They also like closure, meaning, they get great satisfaction from seeing big, important projects being on time. They believe in stabilizing, rather than improvising, and that's exactly what you need if you want to 1) scale and leverage your business (predictably) to its next level, and 2) not be the one to do it (so you can enjoy your life again).

In my case, my husband is my second-in-command/CEO (he's perfectly wired for it), but it can be someone whom you hire.

The key is, they must really fit the bill. This is not the time to put anyone with a warm body or a pulse into this role. They will be dealing with the operations, managing finances, leading the team, holding people and projects accountable, possibly even hiring and firing members of your team for you.

After all the work, blood, sweat and tears, you deserve the best possible person for this role. And so does your business. (And yes, this person will pay for themselves in just a few months because they will allow you to really step into your own brilliance with the newfound time on your hands.)

How will you work together? You, the owner, will specifically focus on creating the big vision, the master plans for the future of the company, the culture and the business development, while this second-in-command will make it all happen with your team, however big or small it currently is. The key is to embrace your opposite roles, and let each other do the thing you do best, while working together hand-in-hand and focusing on leveraging the accountability piece of the business.

Embrace the Scheduled Disappearing Act. The best way to see how well your business can run without you (and start moving away from the day-to-day) is to take a totally unplugged vacation. It will be planned of course, months ahead of time, and you will inform your clients and customers many weeks or months ahead, your team will be briefed extensively as to how to deal with each function of the business without you, to keep it going and making money. This is an opportunity for you to trust your team and your systems.

The more you can rely on your team to follow your new systems and do things according to your operations manual (like a franchise does) the more it will perform the company's daily functions without having you being there to triple check everything, and the closer you'll be to really enjoying some regular uninterrupted downtime, or at least, focusing on things other than the minutiae.

Prepare checklists, resources, plan for worst case scenarios, instruct, teach, coach, and do your best to leave everyone informed and everything set up to run without you. And then, leave your laptop at the office, take the email app off your phone, instruct everyone at the office to only contact you if someone is bleeding (this is a metaphor) and, then breathe. Trust.

You can start with one day, then three days, then a full week, and eventually, you too can begin taking a month off from your business. Perhaps you will choose to travel or to spend more time with your family, or even to write a book or start a new project unrelated to your current business. The choice is yours.

Use the Scheduled Disappearing Act as an experiment, a way to find out what falls through the cracks when you're not there. The longer the completely unplugged vacation, the better. When you come back, use a "what worked, what didn't and what we would do differently next time" exercise to set up more systems and procedures for future Scheduled Disappearing Acts.

When you follow this process, in time, you will be able to take multiple weeks of vacation a year without your computer, and even a month or two off with minimal involvement. Even if you have no intention of ever taking a month off from your own business, put these into practice anyway. It's the ultimate leverage.

You CAN do this!

> **5. Living the million-dollar lifestyle is more about doing things you love than owning countless desirable possessions.**

"There's a real element of wealth that goes with the freedom
to do what you really like to do."
—Dean Jackson

Play the billionaire game. When I was first interested in getting my own business to the seven-figure mark, I dreamed of all the lives I would be changing, but I also dreamed of private jets and private chefs, entertaining my friends on my yacht, and living a lavish lifestyle. And I feel blessed to have experienced a majority of these things.

When I have asked others, *"What is it that you think having a seven-figure business will afford you?"* often they haven't given it much thought. They tend to want "freedom from" rather than "freedom to," meaning, freedom from debt, or freedom from obligations. And for many, they just don't know what they want.

So, I invite them to play a game with me, one that helps them come up with their ideal lifestyle, the "freedom to" part. From my first life coach, I learned to play a game called "The Billionaire Game." It requires you to take a few minutes to make a list of one hundred items that would answer the following questions:

If you woke up tomorrow as an instant billionaire, but still had to work, how would you spend your day, minute-by-minute? What would your lifestyle be like, specifically?

I've played this game several times before and have asked many thousands to play along at my seminars. For many, it includes experiences that revolve around making the usual purchases you would make upon having lots of money in the bank (buying a new watch, a new car, that handbag you may have been coveting your whole life) but also getting the household help (a chef, a driver, etc.).

But something fascinating happened to me the first time I played this game and I have witnessed countless others experience the same fascinating outcome. What people who make this list usually discover is that a lot of the items they long for on their billionaire list are within their reach now.

- More time off to be with loved ones.
- More travel to places on their bucket list.
- A chance to give back or become a philanthropist.
- Healthy food cooked for them.
- More time to read.
- More time to nap.
- More time for hugging the children.
- More time for running on the beach with the dogs.
- The ability to use our time the way we want to use it.

Besides the first "obligatory" signs of newfound success that come with purchasing the big house and the four cars in the driveway, what practically everyone wants are more experiences, *ones they could actually have now!*

These are typically experiences that don't cost an arm and a leg. Usually, they speak to a yearning for freedom of time and location, the ability to spend time with whom we want, when we want, doing what we want. And that doesn't require a million dollars in the bank. It just requires making (bold) decisions to set our lives up to be free *now*.

What many lifestyle entrepreneurs seek is, 1) making a difference through their work (I call this impact) and 2) freedom to do the things they want to do.

And the good news is, you don't need the traditional trappings of success to experience these now.

You can find more time off to be with loved ones, *now*.

You can travel to places on your bucket list, *now*.

You can give back or become a philanthropist, *now*.

You can find ways to have healthy food cooked for you (or available to you), *now*.

You can prioritize time to read, *now*.

You can take more naps, *now*.

You can spend more time hugging the children, *now*.

You can prioritize time for running on the beach with the dogs, *now*.

You can use your time the way you want to use it, *now*.

You don't have to wait UNTIL you have that million-dollar business. It's not mutually exclusive. With a second-in-command, and some strategic changes in your business model, automation, team, and systems, you can begin to live this way now.

It's just a decision. ;)

Your (real) criteria for success may be vastly different from what you currently think it is. As we've been discussing, the key principle around having a Lifestyle Business is that you're looking to create and sustain a specific level of income as the business owner. Nothing else. In other words, its purpose is to provide you with a lovely lifestyle.

Admittedly, this is not what we're talking about here, because we are also looking to scale your business so that it can continue to grow without you. But there is something that we can learn from a pure Lifestyle Business and my dear friend Dean Jackson, defines his own lifestyle success by the following phrase and criteria:

"I know I'm being successful when . . ."

I am able to wake up and ask, *"What do I want to do today?"*

My passive income exceeds my lifestyle needs

I'm working on projects that excite me and allow me to do my very best work

I can live anywhere in the world I choose

I can disappear for several weeks with no effect on my income

There are no whine-y people in my life

I have no time obligations or deadlines

I wear whatever I want, all the time

Those are Dean's criteria for success, his non-negotiables.

This list of criteria for a successful life then becomes a filter through which every decision in the business (important or otherwise) is made. (When Derek and I hadn't yet moved to Paris from the US, our filter through which we made our own decisions about the business or anything in our personal life was "All roads lead to Paris." Meaning, we knew we would be successful when the business ran perfectly even if we were halfway across the world from our team, and that our family was happy.)

An important thing Dean mentions is that there is no right or wrong answer for everyone. And that you should choose your criteria based on how you want to design your lifestyle. Some people need structure and deadlines, for example, while others, like him, do much better by not having the pressure of deadlines.

I've heard of many highly successful business owners who have strict rules as to how they do business. Some of these non-negotiable rules can include never getting on a plane unless it's for pleasure, taking completely unplugged vacations, never having to miss a 10:00 a.m. yoga class, never having to put on pantyhose ever again, never having to wear a suit and tie, never working on evenings and weekends, never being away from your children for more than three "sleeps" in a row, financing the building of a minimum of three new schools in Africa every year, one two-week family trip to Europe each year, taking August and December off every year, taking a two- to three-day "staycation" with your spouse (staying in a hotel across town) to stay connected to each other, etc.

What are *your* non-negotiables to an ideal lifestyle, even if you don't see how you could ever make it work?

And most importantly, what changes could you make over the next twelve to twenty-four months in how you run your business to get closer to a freedom-based lifestyle? (Be bold here.)

In the end, doing the things required to gain your life back is an act of *self-love* and *self-worth*. Remember, you didn't start this business to make less and work more hours than you would find acceptable working for someone else.

This means feeling worthy of beginning to create the lifestyle you crave, *now*, not just later when you've become "a billionaire." In the hamster wheel of life, it can become really confusing to wait until we have all the money in the world to prioritize having what I call an *obscenely high quality of life.*

You are worthy of it.

You always have been.

You have permission to make decisions that serve you.

You don't need to sacrifice your life for your business.

The way to experience it is when you have leveraged your team, your systems, your time, your business model, your marketing, your accountability, your differentiation and that second-in-command who will allow you to have your life back. That's when you get your life back.

I'm also here to tell you that you can just decide to begin the journey to having that obscenely high quality of life now, my sweet friend.

What's the impact of applying the Lifestyle Activator in your business? Judy explains it to you in her own words:

"I'm a financial concierge, bookkeeper to billionaires, certified money coach, and a published author, thanks to this program. For more than 20 years, I ran my business by the seat of my pants. I didn't have any plans, I didn't have any systems. I was just being me and getting out there doing my thing and getting clients. But everything is just different now.

"I have removed myself a lot from the business. I'm working more on my business, thanks to Fabienne. She taught me how to do that instead of working in my business and I've leveraged a lot. This program has opened up a whole new world to me.

"I now have a team, we have systems. We have team meetings now. Everybody's on the same page. I've learned so much. Everything has changed. I don't do any scheduling, any admin and I don't even have to deal with email anymore, my team members do that. We have an operations manual that details everything so now if someone's not there to do something, another member of my staff can just look at the manual and can do it. I never had that in place before.

"The community in the Leveraged Business program is amazing. Not only do I learn from Fabienne and from her process, I learn from everybody else because people are just so generous with their infor-mation. The love that I get from everybody that's in here, it's a family to me. We get together even when we're not in the meeting, and we all hug and love each other and go out and have dinner together. We check in with each other in between.

"I heard about Fabienne about 10 years ago, but I had never invested a penny into my own business, so I hesitated, thinking that, if anything, I needed a private coach instead of a program. If I could turn back the clocks in my business, I would've signed up 10 years ago because I would be a lot further along. Don't wait 10 years. Do it. It's worth it. The community is amazing. The people are amazing. Fabienne is amazing. The love in this program is just phenomenal.

"I've always loved my business, but now I love the way it's running better than it ever did before. It runs smoothly. I can go away on vacation and not worry about it. It's been phenomenal. I feel so much more self confident." —Judy Heft

What's Next For You?

AYBE WE CAN HELP.
From these pages, you've gained some insight on the specific mindset needed to make the changes we discussed. Why mindset first? In my experience, no lasting change (and therefore, no results) can occur without a shift in mindset.

As I have been teaching for more than twenty years, action comes not from the conscious mind (willpower) but from the subconscious realm (beliefs and self-image that make up your mindset). That's why we lead here with mindset shifts.

Once you've put a new belief system in place, it's easy to make pragmatic and tactical changes, so you can achieve a Leveraged Business that brings you to multiple Six and eventually Seven Figures, while gaining an extraordinary quality of life, including freedom, fulfillment, and impact.

So, we've dealt with the mindset. And now, it's time for the tactical, nuts-and-bolts how-to.

Perhaps you've never had the opportunity to build a Seven Figure business. There may be a lot you don't know about the process. That's where we come in.

Helping people like you is what we do day in and day out in the Leveraged Business program.

This is where millionaires are made. With ease and grace, and a community to champion you and give you resources and feedback along the way.

Is the program right for you?

Maybe. Let's see.

If there is a small part of you that feels that you could find success so much faster with our help than alone, perhaps we should chat.

Just as it's difficult to give yourself a good haircut, it's hard for you to see the blind spots in your own business plan. I know that I sometimes lose steam or experience self-doubt when I'm attempting something big by myself, even when I have a high-level road map in front of me.

Conversely, I do really well when someone with more experience tells me, "Do this, and not that."

If you're like me, and the thought of moving forward on your own feels too big, I have two suggestions.

1) Take the Leveraged Business assessment.

The **free Leveraged Business assessment** will show you what's currently stopping you from fully leveraging your business and help you quickly see opportunities for improvement. The assessment takes an average of five minutes to complete, and we'll send you your results once you're done.

To take the Leveraged Business assessment, please go to **www.TheLeverageAssessment.com.**

2) Request a free exploratory session so we can chat about
your business.

Let's book you for a free exploratory session with one of my
seasoned coaches—people who have been through my program for
their own businesses, who understand exactly where you might be
experiencing challenges, and who can help you map out a plan of
action while also exploring with you what it would look like for us
to work together. Book your free session at
www.TheLeveragedBusiness.com.

If you are already at Six or Seven Figures and are overwhelmed—longing to have more consistency, to remove yourself as
the bottleneck of the business, to create more or better systems, to
delegate more effectively, to find someone who can help you with
the day-to-day operations of your business, and to enjoy greater
fulfillment and a much higher quality of life—you will find his
exploratory call very helpful.

Time and time again, I've found that just one conversation can change your life for the better. This may be it. We offer a safe space to discuss aspects of your business that you hesitate to share with others. We're here with a compassionate ear to listen to your particular struggles (with zero judgment, because we've all been there), and to help you find out what's slowing you down.

Go to **www.TheLeveragedBusiness.com** and request the free session, answering a few simple questions. These will get us on our way to solving your problems, and give you more details about the program.

Praise for The Leveraged Business Program

Does the process I outlined in this book really work? Here are some real-life examples from our members:

"I came here with a successful health coaching practice, but I knew that there was a bigger game I was supposed to be playing. I saw so many health coaches struggling to have a six-figure practice, and as a scientist by training, I believe that arming health coaches with clinical knowledge will solve the health-care crisis.

"But I struggled, because the skills I'd used to build my health coaching practice didn't work when I tried to follow this calling. I needed tools and a shift in my mindset.

"In my first year here, I doubled my income in my new business, and now I have hundreds of clients, while being able to leverage my first business. I can't tell you the relief I've experienced by being able to experience this kind of growth without working harder. If anything, I'm working less.

"There is such an incredible love here and an unwavering insistence in this community that we all rise. And we do." —Tracy Harrison

"When I originally began working with Fabienne, my business was more of a hobby. I decided to work with her because I knew I had everything in me to be successful, I just didn't know what to do. I

needed a little help. I needed someone to show me, believe in me, to give me the step-by-step structure, and I needed the community.

"I joined her initial program, where I learned about generating new income, which is exactly what I needed to do when I just started out. It's all about the marketing, believing in myself, and making it happen. From that program, I generated five times more revenue.

"Within six months, I moved up to the Leveraged Business program. And once I did that, I stopped struggling. I started to let go and believe in myself, in my dream, and in the work I do. And now, the exact type of people I want to work with just come to me. I changed who I served, I changed my prices, and I changed my programs. And they keep coming.

"I enjoy every moment of being a business owner, now. Before, it was such a hard job. I loved what I did. I was passionate about what I did. But I would wake up in the morning and think, "Who can I call today to offer my services?" It's not easy. Every day, again and again. And I started to not believe in myself and to doubt myself. And there's no one to talk to.

"Having Fabienne holding my hand is a blessing. My whole world changed when I joined the program. My life as a mom changed. I have time to be with my kids, to pick them up from school, to go to lunch with them and with my husband. I have a team and I take vacations.

"If you have it in your heart, if you know there's something out there for you, don't think. Just do it because Fabienne is going to make it happen for you. She knows this stuff. Let it go and just come." —Sarit Lotem

"I began working with Fabienne about three and a half years ago when it was just me in my business. I was totally maxed out. I *couldn't take on any more clients because there were no more hours in the day. I was working nights and weekends, and I was exhausted. I thought it had to be that way, that it had to always just be me delivering, and that no one else could do it like I do it.*

"As of today, I have eight employees, two businesses, and have started a separate business line. The financial growth from the day I signed up to today is an 800 percent increase in revenue. And I was already at Six Figures when I started.

"I learned how to put a team together. I learned that it's okay to let go. And I learned how to put systems in place so when you do let go, it is still being done my way, my method.

"Probably the biggest thing I've learned in the past three and a half years working in the Leveraged Business program is that I can be this successful and have a life. I can say no. I learned how to dream big, bigger than I ever, ever thought was imaginable. I never would have thought I'd have this success three years ago.

"I'm being stretched every year. Every time Fabienne talks to me, I think, "Oh! Here we go again. What are we going to do now?" And it works every time.

"I have made some of the dearest friends in this community – people that get me and I get them on a level that I just cannot find at home. From our super, super highs, to our really lowest of lows, we're there for each other. We may not speak every week, we may not speak every month sometimes. But gosh, when you need a friend, they are there, they drop everything, and they have your back 100 percent.

"I have had my butt kicked, and I have been hugged like never before in my life. It has been an amazing journey.

"For those of you that are out there working evenings and weekends, who are crushed under your business and overwhelmed, and might even be thinking about just throwing in the towel because it's not worth it: it doesn't have to be this way. (I too thought you had to work hard all the time to be a success.)

"The biggest joke at our business meetings was that I would not submit vacation time because what would happen when I left? The world would fall apart! I now take six weeks of vacation. If I work nights and weekends, it's by my choice, not because I have to or because someone's telling me I do. My life is better. My life is more balanced. And this is pretty freaking awesome." —Terri Bradley

"I own a company in New York City called the Kingston Training Group, and we train business technology sales executives to prospect effectively at the C level with the vertical focus to open up full technology solution opportunities.

"When I first joined, I was a telemarketer making $25 an appointment. I was really good at making meetings—it came easily to me. And as a former actor, I like to be on stage so I thought, 'Why couldn't I help the people that sat next to me?' and became a trainer. I sat down with Fabienne and wrote a workbook. And within four months of joining, I was making $10,000 a month.

"I took a few years off and came back for the Leveraged Business program and I passed the $500,000-per-year mark.

Present day, I am making over $1 million a year. The one thing I know is when I'm around my coaches and peers in the program, I make more money. Period." —Kate Kingston

About the Author

Okay, here's my official blurb, the one I use when booked for speaking engagements:

FABIENNE FREDRICKSON is a powerful catalyst for solo business owners who seek to make a powerful impact in their work, while creating certainty in their businesses and financial security in their lives. What gets her out of bed each morning? She believes that when women make their own money (and lots of it), they experience a profound feeling of safety. That's when they take up more space in their families, their communities, and the world.

For more than twenty years, she has been, and continues to be, a mentor to tens of thousands of women business owners (and men who appreciate learning from a strong woman) as the founder of Boldheart.com, the parent company that now houses her many brands. Her company has repeatedly been recognized by the media, and *Inc.* magazine has named it one of America's fastest-growing private companies for three consecutive years.

She is an inspiring speaker to audiences as large as seven thousand, and has been featured in *Forbes, Entrepreneur, Inc., Fast Company*, American Express OPEN, and *The New York Times*, among other publications.

The Leveraged Business program is based on more than two decades and tens of millions of dollars in results for the more than five hundred members who have gone through the program to date. For more information, free resources including an assessment, member success stories, and to explore what it would be like to become a member of the program, please visit **www. TheLeveragedBusiness.com.**

In everything she does, Fabienne likes to say that she sprinkles self-worth and mindset principles on all of her teachings, as one would sprinkle fairy dust. She teaches you to fight self-doubt, become infinitely more confident, believe in yourself, value your unique brilliance, and then get out of your comfort zone so you can create a life that you love. She teaches these self-worth principles at Fabienne.com.

For more on her personal and lifestyle coaching, you may enjoy reading her book, *Embrace Your Magnificence: Get Out of Your Own Way and Live a Richer, Fuller, More Abundant Life* (published by Hay House), and exploring her Boldheart Life program.

Want to follow Fabienne in real time? You can find her here:

Facebook:	@Fabienne
Instagram:	@FabienneFred
Twitter:	@Fabienne
LinkedIn:	Fabiennefredrickson

But on a more personal front, here's what those who really know me know about me:

I love love.

I'm always up for giving you a big hug.

I believe deeply in personal responsibility.

If I make a mistake, I clean it up.

I can throw a really good party.

I love to dance, but I can't do a line dance for anything—so don't try to get me to do the Macarena or the Hustle, because I won't.

I never say no to champagne, oysters, stinky French cheese, or truffles on anything, even leftover spaghetti.

Dark chocolate is an everyday feature in my life.

I am fiercely loving, but not lenient.

I will go to bat for you when no one else will, and believe in you until you believe in yourself.

I am spiritual and I channel, even in business.

I am deeply in love with my husband, Derek; he is my soul mate, and he makes me laugh every single day.

I have three kids whom I am incredibly proud of: Claire, Luc, and Oliver.

I wear my heart on my sleeve, which means I cry easily, and I am totally fine with that.

I'm funny—really, I am . . . even though my kids say that I only have "humorous tendencies."

Even though I've created a business that generates multiple Seven Figures each year, I am a spiritual teacher and healer. I just happen to offer spiritual support while helping you make lots of money and create a life you love.

I absolutely believe that you can be both spiritual and financially abundant, and that there's nothing wrong with that.

My life's purpose is to activate yours and have you play a much bigger game than you're playing now.

Along with our awesome members, I have helped build over twenty-six schools in the Masai Mara region of Kenya in Africa, and I went there to meet hundreds of "our kids in Kenya" and their parents with my daughter; it was life-changing. I will never be the same as a result.

I live in Paris with my family, just because we want to.

And finally, here's what I, and my entire team, stand for:

We believe in doing everything with authenticity, integrity, and love.

We believe that the things you are passionate about aren't random—they are your calling.

We believe that your potential for greatness is already within you, and that you just need the right environment to grow into it.

We believe that you *are* good enough. There is nothing wrong with you and there never has been.

We believe that everyone is born with a purpose, and that it's our divine duty to use it for good.

We believe in the positive power of entrepreneurship.

We believe in aligning your business with your passions and your unique calling.

We believe in the power of community; we know it's incredibly difficult to do great things by yourself. (And why would you?)

We believe in always being part of a like-minded tribe. As you grow professionally, you will also grow personally, a process that requires the unconditional emotional support and collective wisdom of a group of people who believe in you—more than just one person or coach could ever give you. Tribe is everything.

We believe that it's imperative to deny your feelings of smallness and to redirect the part of you that sometimes feels inadequate and undeserving into "I am here for a reason."

We believe in protecting ourselves against naysayers and people who think too small.

We believe that 95 percent of success is directly related to your mindset.

We believe in being bold, brave, and courageous, because magic never happens within your comfort zone.

We believe that, when given the choice to live either a bland existence or a Technicolor one full of meaning and fulfillment, that, well, there is no choice, really.

We believe in you and your greatness.

Are you with us?